ROLL

of the sons and daughters of the
Anglican Church Clergy throughout the
world and of the Naval and Military
Chaplains of the same who
gave their lives in
the Great War
1914-1918

The Naval & Military Press

ROLL

of the sons and daughters of the Anglican
Church Clergy throughout the world
and of the Naval and Military
Chaplains of the same who
gave their lives in
the Great War
1914-1918

Quæ regio terræ nostri non plena laboris?
With the morn those Angel faces smile,
Which I have loved long since, and lost awhile,
Requiem eternam dona eis Domine et lux perpetua luceat eis

Published by

The Naval & Military Press Ltd
Unit 5 Riverside, Brambleside,
Bellbrook Industrial Estate,
Uckfield, East Sussex,
TN22 1QQ England

Tel: +44 (0) 1825 749494

www.naval-military-press.com
www.nmarchive.com

*In reprinting in facsimile from the original, any imperfections are inevitably reproduced
and the quality may fall short of modern type and cartographic standards.*

PREFACE

I have taken extreme care to compile this Roll as accurately as possible, but it is almost inevitable that there should be omissions and that mistakes should have crept in.

With regard to the former, if such should unfortunately prove to be the case after this book is published, all I can do is to issue a second volume or an appendix to this; with regard to the second, all I can do is to apologise, not for want of care, but for inaccurate information.

I have to thank many correspondents throughout the world for valuable aid.

I have to thank the Colonial Bishops for the great help they have given me, especially those of Canada and New Zealand.

It seems that Colonial records of the Clergy in each Diocese are kept far more accurately than those of the Mother Country.

So far as I have been able to discover, there is not a single Diocese in England that has any official record of Clergy, or sons and daughters of Clergy, who gave their lives in the War, or even served; and very few have imperfect lists, compiled by private individuals, but many have none of any sort or kind, whereas the Colonial Dioceses have every detail even to the number on the grave memorials in each Cemetery.

This lack of official lists in England has rendered my work very laborious.

I have also to thank the Public School authorities for great help.

The Navy and the War Office lists are very accurate, but as no indication of parentage is given, I have been compelled to spend much time in examining many thousands of names.

It is impossible within the limits of this Preface to mention all those who helped me in compiling this Roll, but they know from private correspondence how much I thank them. The various Rolls of Honour have also helped me.

It has been a long and trying task, involving an enormous correspondence reaching all over the world, but at the same time a labour of love, inasmuch as it has been done as a Memorial of all those whom we clergy have loved and lost awhile.

RICHARD USSHER,

Vicar of Westbury,

Brackley, Northants.

ROLL

Surname. Christian Name.   *Father's Name and Parish.*   *Where Died.*   *Date.*

Abbay, Capt. Marmaduke John Norman, 87th Punjabis, Canon Abbay, Rector of Earl Soham, Boulogne, May 10-15.

Abbott, Rev. William David, C.F., Rev. David Wyley Abbott, Vicar of Cardington, Dieppe, Dec. 3-18.

Abbott, Lt. Lionel Pilkington, Leicester Regt., Rev. Arthur Abbott, Vicar of Corby, Mametz Wood, July 14-16.

Abbott, William Ethelbert, Machine Gun Corps, Rev. John Thomas Henry Abbott, Vicar of Mullaghdun, Enniskillen, Peronne, Oct. 3-18.

Abigail, Lt. Edward Arnold, R.M.A., Rev. William James Abigail, of Coonoor, S. India, C.M.S., Dunkirk, Mar. 17-16.

Abraham, Capt. Geoffrey William Popperell, Glamorgan Yeomanry, Bishop of Derby, Port Said, Nov. 19-17.

Adams, 2d. Lt. Charles John Norman, Grenadier Guards, Rev. George Augustus Samuel Adams, Rector of Nettlestead, Rouen, Nov. 14-18.

Adams, Capt. John Goold, Leinster Regt., Archdeacon of Derry, Hill 60, May 4-15.

Adams, Lt. Lestock Handley, Rifle Brigade, Rev. Henry Frederick Spencer Adams, Vicar of Holy Trinity, Redhill, Pacaut Wood, April 22-18.

Adams, Maurice Alwyn, New Zealand E.F., Archdeacon of Kildare, France, May 18-17.

Adams, 2d. Lt. Ernest Geoffrey, Norfolk Regt., Rev. Ernest William Adams, Vicar of St. John's, Bury St. Edmunds, Avebury Wood, June 26-18

Adamson, Lt. Francis Douglas, Border Regt., Rev. Cuthbert Edward Adamson, Rector of Houghton le Spring, Givenchy, Nov. 16-15.

Addenbrooke, 2d. Lt. John Homfray, Manchester Regt., Rev. John Gordon Addenbrooke, Vicar of St. Wenn, Beaumont Hamel, Nov. 16-16.

Addis, Lt. Thomas Henry Liddon, Royal Dublin Fusiliers, Rev. William Edward Addis, Vicar of All Saints, Knightsbridge, Mar. 21-18.

Adolphus, Otto Ernest Augustus, Royal Fusiliers, Rev. Horace Octavius Augustus Adolphus, Vicar of St. John's, West Bromwich, Somme, Nov. 9-16.

Aglionby, Major Arthur Hugh, M.C., R.G.A., Rev. Francis Keyes Aglionby, Rector of Newbold Pacey, Monvaux, November 7-18.

Alderson, Major Reginald Liddon, R.A.F., Canon Alderson of Peterborough, Hull, June 30-18.

Alderson, Capt. Reginald, Lancashire Fusiliers, M.C., Mentioned in Despatches, Rev. Henry Everingham Alderson, Vicar of St. James, Hope, Arras, March 25-18.

Aldous, Capt. Stewart John, Sherwood Foresters, Rev. John Clement Primrose Aldous, Rector of Sywell, St. Eloi, Mar. 25-16.

Aldous, 2d. Lt. Alan Edward, Border Regt., Rev. John Clement Primrose Aldous, Rector of Sywell, Thiepval, July 3-16.

Aldworth, 2d. Lt. Douglas Gilbert Hayward, Royal Berks, Rev. Arthur Ernest Aldworth, Vicar of Laverstock, S.S. Leinster, Oct. 10-18.

Algeo, Capt. Norman, Leinster Regt., Rev. Lewis Algeo, Incumbent of Ardara, Donegal, Tincourt, Nov. 30-17.

Algeo, Capt. William, Dorset Regt., Rev. Frederick Swift Algeo, Rector of Studland, Thiepval, May 17-16.

Alington, 2d. Lt. Geoffrey Hugh, Sussex Regt., Rev. Edward Hugh Alington, of Summerfields, Oxford, Somme, Aug. 9-16.

Allan, 2d. Lt. Frank Cecil, Durham L.I., Rev. Thomas Peter Allan, Vicar of Cramlington, Rouen, Sept. 29-16.

Allan, 2d. Lt. Rev. Henry Somerset, London Regt., Rev. George Alexander Allan, Vicar of Isle Abbots, Etaples, Oct. 2-16.

Allin, 2d. Lt. Harold Wyse, Shropshire L.I., Rev. Alfred Thomas Allin, Vicar of Holbeton, El Arish, Dec. 13-14.

Allpass, 2d. Lt. Edmond Theodore, Sherwood Foresters, Rev. Henry Alfred Allpass, Vicar of Stanway, Gallipoli, August 21-15.

Allpass, 2d. Lt. Henry Blythe King, Essex Regt., Rev. Henry Alfred Allpass, Vicar of Stanway, France, Sept. 16-16.

Amies, Nathaniel George Read, The Buffs, Rev. Nathaniel Jones Miller Stuart Amies, Vicar of Brent, Le Touquet, August 20-15.

Anderson, 2d. Lt. Gerard Rupert Laurie, Cheshire Regt., Prebendary Anderson of St. George's, Hanover Square, La Bassee, Nov. 8-14.

Anderson, Capt. Ralph, Australian I.F., Bishop of Riverina, N.S.W., Westhof, June 8-17.

Andrews, Capt. Christopher Boyd, R.M.L.I., Rev. John Marshall Andrews, Vicar of St. Jude's, London, Gallipoli, May 11-15.

Andrews, 2d. Lt. Francis Nicholas, Royal Irish Rifles, Rev. John Wilson Andrews, Vicar of Trysull, Villers Bocage, Oct. 11-15.

Andrews, Capt. Maynard Percy, West Riding Regt., Rev. Percy Andrews, Vicar of Ash, Bosinghe, August 14-15.

Annesley, Capt. James Ferguson St. John, R.A.M.C., Canon Annesley, of Clogher, Thetford, May 19-17.

Anson, Wilfred Gordon, Gloucester Regt., Rev. Harcourt Suft Anson, Rector of Southover, Houlthust Wood, Oct. 22-17.

Antram, Lt. Herbert Wilkins, R.N.R., Rev. Charles Edward Potts Antram, Vicar of Blean, Submarine K17, Jan. 31-18.

Appleton, Major Francis Martin, South Lancashire Regt., Rev. Richard Appleton, Rector of South Weston, Dec. 6-14.

Arbuthnot, 2d. Lt. Gavin Campbell, N. Staffords, Rev. William Arbuthnot, Vicar of Lea Marston, Gallipoli, Aug. 7-15.

Archer, Lt. John William Butts, The Buffs, Rev. George Archer, Rector of Stilton, Ypres, February 16-15.

Arden, 2d. Lt. Humphrey Warwick, R.G.A., Rev. William Henry Arden, Vicar of Whiteparish, Bailleul, June 6-17.

Armstrong, 2d. Lt. Charles Martin, Dublin Fusiliers, Rev. Chancellor Armstrong, Rector of Kilrush, Beaumont Hamel, February 8-17.

Arnold, Lt. Edward Gladwin, R.F.A., Mentioned in Despatches, Rev. Charles Lowther Arnold, Vicar of Holy Trinity, Fareliam, St. Quintin, Mar. 21-18.

Arnold, 2d. Lt. Alban Charles Phidias, Royal Fusiliers, Rev. Charles Lowther Arnold, Vicar of Holy Trinity, Fareliam, Somme, July 7-16.

Arnold, 2d. Lt. Hugo Cholmondeley, The Buffs, Rev. Henry Abel Arnold, Rector of Wolsingham, Camiers, June 12-17.

Arnold, William Arden Egerton, Australian I.F., Rev. Joseph William Arnold, Vicar of Panmure, Victoria, Mudros, Sept. 17-15.

Arundell, Capt. Reinfred Tatton, 2nd Rajputs, Rev. William Henry Arundell, Rector of Cheriton Fitzpaine, Suez Canal, Feb. 3-16.

Ash, Lt. Basil Drummond, R.N., Rev. Cyril Alfred Drummond Ash, Vicar of Saxton, Off Kirkwall, Sept. 29-14.

Askew, Capt. Henry Adam, Border Regt., Canon Askew, Rector of Greystoke, Sailly, December 19-14.

Askey, 2d. Lt. Cecil Henry Leonard, Lincoln Regt., Rev. Arthur Henry Askew, Rector of Swallow, Amiens, April 5-18.

Astbury, Capt. Thomas Leslie, S. Staffords, Canon Astbury, Vicar of Smethwick, March 21-18.

Astley, Lt. Christopher Basil, Liverpool Regt., Rev. John Henry Astley, of St. James', New Brighton, Rouen, July 27-18.

Atkins, Eric Alwyn, Labour Corps, Rev. Horace John Atkins, Rector of Harrington, Bridgeforth, March 15-18.

Atkins, Lt. Herbert de Carteret, Durham L.I., Rev. Gerard Sanders Atkins, Rector of Kuappagh, Le Treport, Oct. 10-15.

Atkinson, Capt. William Noel, 10th Gurkhas, Rev. Augustus William Atkinson, of Octacamund, Gallipoli, May 29-15.

Atkinson, 2d. Lt. Henry Noel, D.S.O., Cheshire Regt., Canon Atkinson, of Chester, Violaincs, Oct. 22-14.

Atkinson, Lt. Arnold Francis Crossley, R.E., Rev. Francis Atkinson, Blackwater House, Eastbourne, Kirgi, Jan. 22-19.

Atlay, Major Hugh Wordsworth, D.S.O., Mentioned in Despatches, R.F.A., Bishop of Hereford, Ypres, April 11-15.

Auden, Cadet Geoffrey William, R.A.F., Rev. Alfred Millington Auden, Vicar of Church Broughton, London, November 4-18.

Awdry, 2d. Lt. Carol Edward Vere, Munster Fusiliers, Rev. Vere Awdry, Vicar of Ampfield, Etreux, Aug. 28-14.

Babington, Humfrey Temple, Australian I.F., Rev. John Albert Babington, Vicar of Tenterden, France, May 1-17.

Back, Rev. Hatfield Arthur William, Naval Chaplain, Rev. Arthur James Back, Rector of Carleton Rode, H.M.S. Vanguard, July 9-17.

Badcock, Lt. Arthur Lawrence, Yorkshire L.I., Rev. Thomas Badcock, Rector of Walgrave, St. Eloi, Oct. 14-15.

Badcock, Lt. Edmund Downes, Northants Regt., Rev. Thomas Badcock, Rector of Walgrave, Contalmaison, July 22-16.

Badham, Lt. Francis Molyneux, R.N.V.R., Rev. Frederick John Badham, Rector of Kilbixy, Westmeath, Gallipoli, June 4-15.

Bagshawe, Capt. Leonard Vale, King's Own Scottish Borderers, Rev. William Augustus Edward Vale Badshawe, Rector of Pitchford, Ypres. June 16-15.

Baile, Lt. Robert Carlyle, R.E., Rev, George William Baile, Consular Chaplain, Pernambuco, Loos, Oct. 24-15.

Bailey, 2d. Lt. John Winckworth, R.A.F., Rev. John Bailey of Rochester, Northolt, March 31-16.

Bailie, Lt. George Richard Lancelot, Inniskilling Fusiliers, Rev. William Bailie, Rector of St. Matthias, Dublin, Le Catelot, Oct. 3-18.

Baillie, Lt. Humphrey John, M.C., Dorset Regt., Rev. William Gordon Baillie, Vicar of Lynton, Kut, March 2-16.

Baillie, Lt. R. G., A.A.F.

Bainbrigge, 2d. Lt. Philip Gillespie, Lancashire Fusiliers, Prebendary Bainbrigge, Sept. 18-18.

Baines, Capt. Arthur Edward Carrow, Lincolnshire Regt., Mentioned in Despatches, Rev. Charles Frederick Baines, Rector of St. Ninian's, Castle Douglas, Mesopotamia, April 9-16.

Baker, Major Roger Dyke, East Lancashire Regt., Rev. Henry Defoe Baker, Rector of Thruxton, Gallipoli, Aug. 13-15.

Baker, Lt. Basil Howard, Rifle Brigade, Rev. Samuel Howard Baker, Vicar of Chesterton, Mesnil Bouche, May 22-18.

Baldwin, Capt. George C. de Courcy, Munster Fusiliers, Rev. W. H. de Courcy Baldwin, Rector of Holtby, France, Jan. 25-16.

Baldwin, Cuthbert Godfrey, R.A.F., Rev. Alan Godfrey Baldwin, Vicar of Burnopfield, Beaumont Hamel, Nov. 3-16.

Bambridge, 2d, Lt. Bertram Stacpoole, East Kent, Canon Bambridge of Canterbury, Grandcourt, March 6-17.

Barber, Major Cyril Frederick, R.M.L.J., Archdeacon of Chester, H.M.S. Goliath, Aug. 2-15.

Baring, 2d. Lt. Cecil Christopher, R. West Kent, Rev. Francis Henry Baring, Rector of Eggesford, March 21-18.

Baring, 2d. Lt. Reginald Arthur, R.A.F., Rev. Francis Henry Baring, Rector of Eggesford, July -18.

Barker, Capt. William Harald, R.G.A., Canon Barker of Kilbroney, Co. Down, Gallipoli, Nov. 5-15.

Barker, Capt. Richard Vincent, Royal Welsh Fusiliers, Rev. Frederick Barker, Rector of Wimborne St. Giles', Ypres, Oct. 31-14.

Barlow, Lt. Theodore Kenneth, S. Stafford Regt. Canon Barlow, Rector of Lawford, Somme, July 15-16.

Barnard, G R Rev. Gilbert William Barnard, of Canford.

Baron, Sub. Lt. Maurice Nelson, R.N.A.S., Rev. Charles William Baron, Rector of Barsham, Nieuport, Aug. 15-17.

Barr, Perceval Stanley St. John, Canadian E.F., Rev. George Barr, Vicar of Cropredy, Ypres, July 9-16.

Barrett, Lt. George, Warwickshire Regt., Rev. Benjamin Barrett, Vicar of Braunston, Gallipoli, Aug. 16-15.

Barrow, 2d. Lt. Laurence Alfred Howard, Royal Sussex Regt., Rev. Alfred Henry Barrow, Vicar of Flamstead, Albert, Aug. 3-16.

Bartlett, Capt. Robert Nigel Oldfeld, East Lancashire Regt., Rev. Charles Oldfeld Bartlett, Vicar of Minsterworth, Mesopotamia, Ap. 6-15.

Barton, Lt. Alfred Richard, South African Infantry, Rev. Alfred John Barton, Rector of Strumpshaw, Delville Wood, July 18-16.

Barton, 2d. Lt. Hugh Fabian, Norfolk Regt., Rev. Alfred John Barton, Rector of Strumpshaw, Ypres, Feb. 12-16.

Bashford, Charles, Rev. Robert Bashford, Rector of St. Mary's, Colchester, -16.

Bass, Capt. Charles Harold, Lancashire Fusiliers, Rev. Charles Bass, Rector of Steeple Claydon, Cambrai, Aug. 26-14.

Bates, Captain William George Henry, Leinster Regt., Rev. William Wheatley Bates of Toronto, Ypres, Ap. 26-15.

Batson, 2nd. Lt. Leonard Henry, East Kent Regt., Rev. Vincent Lascelles Batson, Vicar of Brockland, Somme, July 3-16.

Beanland, Lt. Joseph Wilfrid, Royal Welsh Fusiliers, Rev. Joseph Beanland, Vicar of Skirbeck, Gallipoli, Aug. 10-15.

Beardsworth, Reginald John, Canadian E.F., Rev. John Edward Beardsworth, Vicar of Harbury, Oppy Wood, May 3-17.

Beauchamp, Lt. Montague Barclay Granville, Norfolk Regt., Rev. Sir Montague Harry Procter Beauchamp, Bart., Vicar of Monkton Combe, Gallipoli, Aug. 12-15.

Becher, Capt. Henry Owen Dabridgecourt, Cameronians, Rev. Harry Becher, Rector of Rosscarberry, Bois Grenier, March 13-15.

Beechey, Barnard Reeve, Lincolnshire Regt., Rev. Prince William Thomas Beechey, Rector of Freisthorpe. Unknown, Sept. 25-15.

Beechey, Charles Reeve, Royal Fusiliers, Rev. Prince William Thomas Beechey, Rector of Freisthorpe, East Africa, Oct. 20-17.

Beechey, 2d. Lt. Frank Collett Reeve, E. Yorkshire Regt., Rev. Prince William Thomas Beechey, Rector of Freisthorpe, Warlincourt, Nov. 14-16.

Beechey, Harold Reeve, Australian I.F., Rev. Prince William Thomas Beechey, Rector of Freisthorpe, Arras, Ap. 10-17.

Beechey, Leonard Reeve, London Irish Regt., Rev. Prince William Thomas Beechey, Rector of Freisthorpe. Rouen, Dec. 29-17.

Begg, Lt. Alexander James Bartlet, Northumberland Fusiliers, M.C., Rev. Alexander Begg, Rector of Usworth, March 21-18.

Belcher, Lt. Humphrey Gilbert, Wilts Regt., Rev. Gilbert Edward Belcher, Rector of Chaldon, Gallipoli, Aug. 7-15.

Belcher, Capt. Austin Charles Sandham, Wilts Regt., Rev. Gilbert Edward Belcher, Rector of Chaldon, Gallipoli, Aug. 10-15.

Belcher, Lt.-Col. Harold Thomas, D.S.O., R.F.A., Rev. Thomas Hayes Belcher, Rector of Bramley, July 8-17.

Belcher, Major Raymond Douglas, D.S.O., M.C., F.R.A., Rev. Thomas Hayes Belcher, Rector of Bramley, Le Trepot, Dec. 7-17.

Belcher, Capt. Gordon, M.C., Royal Berks, Rev. Thomas Hayes Belcher, Rector of Bramley, Festubert, May 16-15.

Bell, Lt. Benedict Godfrey Allen, R.A.F., Canon Bell of Norwich, Ap. 7-18.

Bell, 2d. Lt. James Donald Allen, Manchester Fusiliers, Canon Bell of Norwich, March 21-18.

Bell, Rev. Charles Henry, C.F., M.C., Royal Berks Regt., Canon James Bell of Kettlethorpe, Moyenneville, Aug. 23-18.

Bell, Capt. Henry Urmston Bainbridge, R.A.S.C., Canon Bell, Rector of Cheltenham, London, June 6-17.

Bennett, Lt., O.H Dampier, R.A.F., Rev. Owen Cyril Dampier Bennett, Rector of Abberley.

Bennett, 2d. Lt. Reginald, Gloucestershire Regt., Rev. Joseph Bennett, Vicar of Stranton, Beaumont Hamel, Sept. 3-16.

Bennett, Joseph Victor, Royal Berkshires, Rev. William Bennett, Vicar of Kirkham, Carnoy, Aug. 26-18.

Bennetts, Sub. Lt. Eric Augustine, R.A.F., Rev. Thomas Bennetts, Rector of Lifton, Wangles, Aug. 17-17.

Benson, Lt Thomas Brookes, Royal Scots Fusiliers, Rev. Riou George Benson, Rector of Hope Bowdler, Neuve Chapelle, March 12-16.

Beresford, Lt. Col. Rev. Percy William, D.S.O., Mentioned in Despatches, London Regt., Poelcaple, Oct. 26-17.

Bernard, Lt. Robert, Dublin Fusiliers, Archbishop of Dublin, Gallipoli, Ap. 26-15.

Berridge, Lt. Jesse Dell, J.M.C., R.E., Rev. Jesse Berridge, Rector of Little Baddow, Arras, May 24-18.

Berry, Capt. Edward Fleetwood, 9th Gurkhas, Rev. James Fleetwood Berry, Rector of Galway, Mesopotamia, Ap. 17-16.

Bertie, Lt. Ninian Mark Kerr, K.R.R.C., Hon. and Rev. Alberic Edward Bertie, Rector of Gelding, Hooge, May 8-15.

Besley, Capt. Barton Hope, Devonshire Regt., Rev. W. Blundell Besley of Ivedon, Givenchy, Oct. 25-14.

Betts, Lt. Henry Lee, Royal Fusiliers, Rev. John Arthur Betts, Rector of Stokesby, Zillebeke, Sept. 20-17.

Betts, Captain John Hamilton, Manchester Regt., Rev. John Arthur Betts, Rector of Stokesby, Albert, July 7-10.

Beven, 2d. Lt. Thomas, South Lancashire Regt., Rev. Sydney Beven of Brighton, Thiepval, July 4-16.

Bevis, Rev. Henry Bevis, Vicar of Arlingham.

Bickersteth, Capt. Stanley Morris, W. Yorkshire Regt., Rev. Samuel Bickersteth, Vicar of Leeds, Serre, July 1-16.

Billing, Capt. Charles George, R.M.L.I., Rev. George Billing, Vicar of Sturry, Gallipoli, March 10-15.

Binney, Lt. Edward Hibbert, Sherwood Foresters, Rev. John Edward Hibbert Binney, Vicar of H. Trinity, Folkestone, Neuve Chapelle, Oct. 11-17.

Bird, Lt. Wilfrid Stanley, K.R.R.C., Rev. Henry George Bird, Rector of Newdigate, Richebourg St. Avaast, May 9-15.

Birrell, Capt. Stuart Erskine, Somerset L.I., Rev. Erskine Alexander Birrell, Vicar of Kirdford, Hooge, July 11-16.

Blackett, 2d. Lt. Charles Robert, Shropshire L.I., William Robert Blackett, Rector of Smethcote, Ypres, Ap. 26-15.

Blackledge, Cadet William Gregson, Rev. Robert Thomas Blackledge, Rector of Christ Church, Denton, Bristol, May 3-16.

Blake, Capt. James Robert, Worcester Regt., Canon Blake, Vicar of Bretforton Courcelles, March 25-18.

Blake, Edward Sylvester, London University, O.T.C. Artillery, Ealing, March 9-16.

Blakeney,

Blakeston, Bernard Moore, Rev. Luke Harrison Blakeston, Vicar of Womersley, Pontefract.

Bland, Capt. Charles Edward, Hants Regt., Rev. Frederick Charles Bland, Vicar of Milland, Sept. 9-16.

Blandford, William Arthur Innocens, Northumberland Fusiliers, Rev. William Mohne Blandford, Vicar of Sutton, Contaltmaison, Oct. 26-17.

Blaxland, Capt. John Bruce, South Wales Borderers, Rev. Bruce Blaxland, Vicar of The Abbey, Shrewsbury, Kut, Jan. 24-17.

Blencowe, 2d. Lt. Lawrence Cave, Liverpool Regt., Rev. Charles Edward Blencowe, Rector of Marston St. Lawrence, Bois Grenier, June 29-17.

Blencowe, 2d. Lt. Oswald Charles, Oxford & Bucks L.I., Rev. Charles Edward Blencowe, Rector of Marston St Lawrence, Somme, Oct. 10-16.

Bligh, Lt. Edward, Henry Swinburne, R.N.D., Hon and Rev. Henry Bligh, Canon of Winchester, Gallipoli, Sept. 10-15.

Blogg, Major Edward Basil, R.E., D.S.O., Rev. Fowler Dabington Blogg, Rector of Gt. Mongeham, Bethune, March 16-16.

Blythe, Capt. Reginald Crommelin Popham, Gloucester Regt., Bishop in Jerusalem, Gallipoli, June 4-15.

Booking, 2d. Lt. Bernard, East Yorkshire Regt., M.C., Rev. John Child Booking, Vicar of Gnosall, Nieppe Forest, Aug. 21-18.

Booking, 2d. Lt. John Webb, King's Own Yorkshire, Croix de Guerre, Rev. John Child Booking, Vicar of Gnosall, France, Ap. 24-18.

Bodington, Capt. Cecil Herbert, Royal Horse Guards, Rev. Herbert James Bodington, Vicar of Upton-Grey, Arras, Ap. 11-17.

Boissier, Lt. William Arthur Marshall, R.M.A., Rev. Frederick Scobell Boissier, Vicar of Denby, Oesthoek, July 27-17.

Boles, Lt. Noel Henry, Dorset Regt., Canon Boles of Truro, Cape Hellas, Jan. 11-16.

Bolland, 2d. Lt. John Wulstan Charles, Norfolk Regt., Rev. William Ernest Bolland, Rector of Denton, Arras, Ap. 9-17.

Bolton, Lt. Herbert Frederick, South Lancashire Regt., Rev. Frederick Bolton, Vicar of St. George's, Darwen, Fampoux, May 3-17.

Borissow, Ernest, R.A.M.C., Rev. Louis Borrissow, Rector of East Gilling, Mudros, Oct. 8-15.

Borton, Major Cyprian Edward, Malay State Guides, Rev. Neville Arthur Blachley Borton, Rector of Burwell, Imad, Aug. 2-17.

Bosanquet, Capt. Armitage Percy, M.C., Duke of Cornwall's L.I., Rev. Claud Charles Courthope Bosanquet, Vicar of St. Stephen's by Saltash, Cornwall, Hai River, Jan. 5-17.

Botfield, Capt. Charles Sidney Garnett, Bedfordshire Regt., Mentioned in Despatches, Rev. Charles Ramsay Garnett Botfield, Vicar of Moreton, Boulogne, Dec. 14-14.

Botham, Major George Hallam, Northumberland Fusiliers, Rev. George William Botham, Rector of Anderby, Albert, Aug. 3-16.

Bott, Lt. Francis George, Scinde Horse, Rev. William Ernest Bott, Rector of Partney, Basra, Aug. 20-20.

Bott, Capt. William Ernest, Royal Fusiliers, Rev. William Ernest Bott, Rector of Partney, Ephey, Sept. 18-18.

Bott, 2d. Lt. Charles Stuart, Lincolnshire Regt., Rev. William Ernest Bott, Rector of Partney, Feuchy, Ap. 17-17.

Bott, 2d. Lt. George, Rifle Brigade, Rev. Richard Bott, Vicar of Cotehill, Loos, Feb. 9-17.

Boucher, Capt. Alan Estcourt, Leicestershire Regt., Canoe Boucher, Rector of Fro'esworth, Menin, Sept. 25—17.

Boughey, Lt. Anchitel Edward Fletcher, Rifle Brigade, Rev. Anchitel Harry Fletcher Boughey, Vicar of St. Mary the Great, Cambridge, S.S. Leinster, Oct. 10-18.

Boultbee, Lt. Arthur Elsdale, R.A.F., Rev. Frederick Croxall Boultbee, Rector of Hargrave, Pont a Verdun, March 17-17.

Boultbee, Joseph Maxwell, Canadian E.F., Rev. Frederick Croxall Boultbee, Rector of Hargrave, Ypres, Ap. 22-15.

Bourne, 2d. Lt. Austen Spencer, South Staffordshire Regt., Rev. Alfred Ernest Bourne, Vicar of Sutton-at-Hone, Monchy, Ap. 23-17.

Bourne 2d. Lt. Cyprian, West Surrey Regt., Rev. Stephen Eugene Bourne, Vicar of Dunston, Arras, Ap. 11-17.

Bourne, 2d. Lt. John Callender, Worcester Regt., Rev. Joseph Handforth Bourne, Rector of Broome, Gallipoli, July 18-15.

Bowden, Lt. John Desborough, N.Z.E.F., Rev. Charles S. Bowden, Vicar of Riccarton, N.Z., Heilly, Oct. 10-16.

Bowen, Lt. Cuthbert Edward Latimer, King's African Rifles, Rev. Thomas James Bowen, Vicar of St. Nicholas, Bristol, Kissi, Dec. 1-14.

Bowen, Major George Eustace Summers, M.C., R.F.A., Rev. Thomas James Bowen, Vicar of St, Nicholas, Bristol, Poperinghe, July 26-17.

Bowlby, Capt. George Elliott Lowes, Lincolnshire Regt., Rev. Alfred Elliott Bowlby, Vicar of St. James', West Streatham, Armentieres, March 15-16.

Bowles, Lt. Reginald Julian Albany, Royal Welsh Fusiliers, Rev. Henry Albany Bowles, Vicar of Christ Church, Epsom, Corbie, July 20-16.

Boyce, Innes Douglas, Royal Berks, Rev. Wilfrid Anderdon Boyce, Rector of Litchfield, Poelvillers, Aug. 16-16.

Bradley, Lt.-Col. Frederick Hoysted, R.A.M.C., D.S.O., Cannon Bradley of Monaghan, Bapaume, Sept. 22-18.

Brain, Edward George, Australian I.F., Rev. Alfred Brain, Rector of Korumburra, Victoria, Gallipoli, Oct. 24-15.

Braithwaite, Major Francis Joseph, North Lancashire Regt., Rev. Francis Joseph Braithwaite, Rector of Gt. Waldingfield, Tanga, East Africa, Nov. 4-14.

Braithwaite, 2d. Lt. Humphry Layland, R.E., Rev. Francis Joseph Braithwaite, Rector of Gt. Waldingfield, Plogstreet, July 10-16.

Braithwaite, Capt. Philip Pipon, Jacobs Horse, Rev. Philip Richard Pipon Braithwaite, Canon of Winchester, Beisan, Palestine, Sep. 23-17.

Bramley, Capt. Cyril Richard, Yorkshire Regt., Rev. Cyril Richard Bramley, Vicar of Donisthorpe, Beaumont Hamel, Feb. 20-17.

Bramley, Lt. Harold, Yorkshire Regt., Rev. Cyril Richard Bramley, Vicar of Donisthorpe, Ypres, May 13-15.

Brandram, 2d. Lt. Christopher, London Regt., Rev. J. Brandram, C.M.S, Japan, France, Sept. 1-18.

Bree, Lt. Edward Russell Stapylton, Duke of Cornwall's L.I., Rev. Edward Henry Bree, Rector of Stow Maries, Dora Tepe, Sept. 18-18.

Bren, Lt. Henry Alfred Hogarth, Leinster Regt., Rev. Henry Alfred Bren, Training College, Cheltenham, Ginchy, Sept. 9-16.

Brodrick, Lt. Eric William, Yorkshire Regt., Rev. Francis Edward Brodrick, Rector of Farnley, Warwick, July 23-16.

Bromehead, Rev. John Nowill Bromehead, Rector of Beverston.

Brooking, Capt. Hugh Cyril Arthur, North Somerset Yeomanry, Rev. Arthur Conolly Brooking, Vicar of Bovington, Purfleet, Aug. 31-18.

Brown, Lt. Arthur Kennish, Canadian E.F., Rev. William Cowell Brown, Festubert, May 23-15,

Brown, Capt. David Hepburn, Scottish Borderers, Rev. David Hepburn Brown, Rector of Harrismith, Le Bassee, Sept. 26-15.

Brown, Lt. Ernest Edward, Wilts Regt., Rev. Albert Edward Brown, Vicar of Alstonefield, Arras, May 9-16.

Brown, Wilfrid, Gloucester Regt., Rev. Albert Edward Brown, Vicar of Alstonefield, Somme, July 3-16.

Brown, George Henry Jennings, Middlesex Regt., Rev. Thomas Brown, Vicar of St. Stephen's, Walthamstow, Jan. 16-16.

Brown, Rev. Guy Spencer Bryan, Chaplain, New Zealand E.F., Rev Willoughby Bryan Brown of St. Stephen's, Eastbourne, Paschendaele, Oct. 4-18.

Brown, 2d. Lt. John Cuthbert Backhouse, Middlesex Regt., Rev. Alexander Brown, Vicar of Buningyon, Victoria, Sept. 29-18.

Browne, Lt.-Col. Eric Anthony Rollo Gore, King's African Rifles, Rev. Robert Melvill Gore Browne, Rector of Leckhampstead, East Africa, July 3-18.

Browne, Harold Rollo Gore, Assistant Paymaster, R.N., H.M.S. Invincible, Rev. Robert Melvill Gore Browne, Rector of Leckhampstead, Jutland, May 31-16.

Browne, Major Frederick Macdonnell, R.E., Archdeacon of Madras, Bethune, Oct. 11-15.

Browne, Major Geoffrey Dennis, R.F.A., Rev Ernest Alfred Browne of Clifton, Ovillers, Sept. 19-16,

Browne, Lt.-Com. Granville Murray, R.N., Rev. Charles Chapman Murray Browne, Vicar of Hucclecote, H.M.S. Indefatigable, Jutland, May 31-16.

Browne, Orde Murray, Canadian E.F., Rev. Charles Chapman Murray Browne, Vicar of Hucclecote, Ypres, June 14-16.

Bruce, Lt. Robert Lloyd, Cameronians, Rev. Robert Douglas Bruce, The Rectory, Dunbar, Serbia, Nov. 18-19.

Bratton, Lt. Eric West, M.C., Devonshire Regt., Rev. Ernest Bartholomew Bratton, Vicar of Aylesbeare, Neuve Eglise, Ap. 14-18.

Buckland, 2d. Lt. John Arnold, Somerset L. I., Rev. John Vansittart Buckland, Rector of Whitelackington, Sailly, March 1-17

Buckley, Capt. Humphrey Paul Stennett, East Yorkshire Regt., Rev. Eric Rede Buckley, Vicar of Burley in Wharfedale, Roeux, July 28-17,

Buckmaster, 2d. Lt. Henry Augustine, L. North Lancashire Regt., Rev. Charles John Buckmaster, Vicar of Hindley, Cambrai, Sept. 28-18.

Buckmaster, Capt. Ralph Nevill Lendon, L. North Lancashire Regt., Rev. Charles John Buckmaster, Vicar of Hindley, Epehy, Nov. 30-17,

Bucknall, 2d. Lt. Marc Anthony, Duke of Cornwall's L.I., Rev. Marc Anthony Bucknall, Vicar of St. Winnow, Unknown, March 6-17.

Bulkeley, Capt. Llewelyn Alfred Henry, R.A.M.C., Canon Bulkeley of Coddington, Bouzincourt, Ap. 10-18.

Buller, Frederick Derrick Edwin, East African Mounted Rifles, Rev. F. George Buller, Rector of Ockford, East Africa, Sept. 25-14.

Bulmer, 2d. Lt. John Legg, Oxford & Bucks L.I., Rev. Edward Buhner, Rector of St. Martin, York, Arras, May 3-17.

Burges, 2d. Lt. Eric Laurence Arthur Hart, Wilts Regt., Rev. T. Hart Burges, Rector of Devizes, Reutel, Oct. 23-14.

Burgess, John Donald, East African Mounted Rifles, Rev Sanuel Burgess of Edgbaston, East Africa, Sept. 25-14.

Burgh, Lt. Edward Henry, M.C., R.F.A., Rev. Henry Ulysses Burgh, Vicar of Preston Patrick, Trescault, Jan. 4-18.

Burn, 2d. Lt. Arthur Sidney Pelham, Mentioned in Despatches, Gordon Highlanders, Archdeacon of Norfolk, Festubert, May 2-15.

Burn, Lt. Maurice Edward Pelham, Black Watch, Archdeacon of Norfolk, Vimy Ridge, Ap. 9-17.

Burn, Capt. Cuthbert, Leicester Regt., Bishop of Quappelle, Poly-gon Wood, Oct. 1-17.

Burnaby, Lt. Geoffrey, London Regt., Rev. John Charles Wellesley, Burnaby, Rector of Asfordly, Somme, Oct. 23-16.

Burnaby, Lt.-Col. Hugo Beaumont, D.S.O., Royal West Surrey, Rev. S. J3. Burnaby, Vicar of Hamstead, Sept. 8-16.

Burr, 2d. Lt. Frederick Bonham, Worcester Regt., Rev. George Frederick Burr, of Meriden, Kemmel, March 12-15.

Burrell, Lt. Stanley Walter, R.A.M.C., Rev. Frederick Walter Isaacs (he took the name of Burrell), Prebendary of St. Paul's, Vicar of Chiswick, July 22-16.

Burrows, 2d. Lt. Leonard Righton, Northumberland Fusiliers, Bishop of Sheffield, Hill 60, Oct, 2-15.

Burton, Harry Pether, 30th Battery Australian I.F., Rev. Alfred Burton, Rector of Swan, West Australia, Somme, Ap. 24-18.

Bury, Wilfrid Entwisle, Canadian E.F., Rev. Edward Bury, Vicar of New Ferry, Passchendale, Nov. 15-17.

Bush, Lt. James Cromwell, M.C., R.A.F., Rev. Herbert Cromwell Bush of Seend, Neuville, Oct. 7-17.

Bussell, Capt. Rev. John Garratt, Sussex Regt., Rev. John Garratt Bussell, Vicar of Balderton, Flanders, June 28-15.

Butler, Lt. Armar Somerset, South Lancashire Regt., att. Wilts, Rev. Pierce Armar Butler, Vicar of Winterslow, Macedonia, Oct. 16-17.

Butler, Lt. John Ormonde, R.A.F., Rev. Robert Moore Peile Butler, Rector of Priston, Mons, Ap. 11-18.

Butler, Paymaster Ralph Twisden, R.N., Rev. Pierce Armar Butler, Vicar of Winterslow, H.M.S. Hampshire, June 5-16.

Butler, Noel, 2d. Lt. Irish Guards, Rev. George Henry Butler, Rector of Knipton, Sept. 15-16.

Cadogan, Lt.-Col. Henry Osbert Samuel, Royal Welsh Fusiliers, Rev. Edward Cadogan, Rector of Wicken, Ypres, Oct. 30-14.

Caldecott, Lt. John Leslie, R.G.A., Rev. Andrew Caldecott, Rector of West Chiltington, Kasoa, Sept. 19-14.

Caldwell, Lt. Gavin Ralston Mure, Coldstream Guards, Rev. William Henry McKennal Caldwell, Rector of Fetcham, Cambrai, Sept. 9-18.

Caley, Capt. Vernon Christopher Russell, Royal Warwicks, Rev. William Bertram Russell Caley, Vicar of Havering-atte-Bower, Ypres, Aug. 22-17.

Calley, Lt. Oliver John, Wilts Regt., Rev. John Henry Calley, Vicar of Figheldean, Spanbrock, March 12-15.

Callinan, 2d. Lt. Thomas William, Durham L.I., Rev. Thomas Callinan, Vicar of Bearpark, St Julien, Apr. 25-15.

Cambie, Lt. Edward Maurice Edwin, Yorkshire L.I., Rev. Solomon Richard Cambie, Rector of Otley, Hebuterne, July 1-16.

Cameron, 2d. Lt. Arthur Ian Douglas, Seaforth Highlanders, Rev. Angus Cameron of St. Andrews, Tain, St. Julien, Apr. 23-15.

Campbell, Capt. Donald William Auchinbreck, South Staffordshire Regt., Rev. William Pitcairn Auchinbreck Campbell, Rector of Fladbury, Neuve Chapelle, Nov. 22-14.

Campbell, Lt. Malcolm Dring, R.N.V.R., Canon Campbell of Carlisle, Gallipoli, Oct. 8-15.

Campbell, Lt. T. C., R.E., Rev. William Howard Campbell, Missionary in Cuddapale, Gallipoli, Oct. 8-15.

Cane, Capt. Lionel Alfred Francis, East Lancashire Regt., Rev. Alfred Granger Cane, Vicar of Paxton, Ploegsteert Wood, Nov. 7-14.

Capell, Capt. Arthur George Coningsby, Northants Regt., Rev. George Marie Capell, Rector of Passenham, Neuve Chapelle, March 12-15.

Cardew, Rev. William Berry Cardew, Vicar of Perlethorpe,

Carew, 2d. Lt. Jasper, West Yorkshire Regt., Rev. Henry Carew, Vicar of Rattery, Hazebronck, Oct. 14-14.

Carpenter, Capt. Edward Berry, R.M.L.I., Rev. Edward Stanley Carpenter, Vicar of Highcliffe, Gallipoli, Aug. 18-15.

Carpenter, Lt. John Phillip Morton, R.F.A., Archdeacon of Sarum, Somme, Sept. 16-16.

Carré, Lt. Edward Mervyn, Lincolnshire Regt., Rev. Arthur Augustus Carré, Rector of Smarden, Hebuterne, Oct. 16-16.

Carré, Capt. Gilbert Trenchard, West Kent Regt., Rev. Arthur Augustus Carré, Rector of Smarden, Cambrai, Nov. 20-17.

Carré, Maurice Tennant, Australian I.F., Rev. Arthur Augustus Carré, Rector of Smarden, Gallipoli, Sep. 2-15.

Carrington, Capt. Christopher, N.Z.E.F., Dean of Christchurch, N.Z., Flers, Oct. 8-16.

Carter, 2d. Lt. Bernard Robert Hadow, R.A.F., Rev. James Octavius Holderness Carter, Rector of Slymbridge, Anglesea, Nov. 7-17.

Carter, Clement Cyril, Worcester Regt., Rev. William David Carter of St. John's, Stand Lane, Hooge, July 21-17.

Carter, Capt. Edward Maurice, 11th Bengal Lancers, Rev. George Charles Carter, Rector of Bartlow, Tel Afar, Mesopotamia, Aug. 11-20.

Cartwright, 2d. Lt. John Digby, Durham L.I., Rev. William Digby Cartwright, Rector of Aynhoe, Hooge, Aug. 19-15.

Cartwright, 2d. Lt. Nigel Walter Henry, Durham L.I., Rev. William Digby Cartwright, Rector of Aynhoe, Ypres, Sept. 21-17.

Carver, 2d. Lt. Lionel Henry Liptrap, Irish Guards, Rev. Henry Jonathan Carver, Rector of Melbury Abbas, Arras, March 26-18.

Case, Lt. John Monckton, Canadian E.F., Rev. F. Case, Sandwich, Dec. 9-17.

Cass, Capt. Leonard Francis, Sussex Regt., Rev. William Anthony Cass, Vicar of Burford, Flanders, Dec. 13-15.

Causton, Capt. Jervoise Purefoy, Hampshire Regt., Rev. Francis Jervoise Causton, Master of St. Cross, Winchester, Pacaud Wood, Apr. 22-18.

Cave, Capt. Bernard Cave Browne Cave, Wilts Regt., Rev. Ambrose Sneyd Cave Browne Cave, Rector of Stretton en le Field, Apr. 5-17.

Cawood, Capt. William Benjamin Crane, R.F.A., Rev. John Cawood, Vicar of Hamble, Mhow, May 24-15.

Cecil, Lt. Randle William Gascoyne, Warwickshire R.H.A., Bishop of Exeter, Mesnieres, Dec. 1-16.

Cecil, Capt. John Arthur Gascoyne, M.C., R.F.A., Bishop of Exeter, Mory, Aug. 27-18.

Cecil, Lt. Rupert Edward Gascoyne, Bedfordshire Regt., Bishop of Exeter, Ypres, July 11-15.

Chambers, James Haxton Foster, Australian I.F., Rev. Charles James Chambers, Vicar of Smithtown, N.S.W., Peronne, Sept. 18-18.

Champion, Lt. Christopher Henry Duncan, Australian I.F., Rev. Arthur Hammerton Champion, Rector of Bungendore, N.S.W., Strazeele, Apr. 14-18.

Champion, Lt. Geoffrey Servante, Australian I.F., Rev. Arthur Hammerton Champion, Rector of Bungendore, N.S.W., Pozieres, July 25-15.

Chapman, Alfred Reginald Bewes, Lancashire N. Regt., Bishop of Colchester, Arras, June 6-16.

Chapman, Capt. Gordon Humphrey, 53rd Sikhs, Rev. Theodore Charles Chapman, Rector of Langley, Kut, March 9-16.

Chapman, Capt. Perceval Christian, R.G.A., Rev. Theodore Charles Chapman, Rector of Langley, Alexandria, May 1-15.

Chapman, Capt. Theodore Victor, M.C., West Surrey Regt., Rev. Theodore Charles Chapman, Rector of Langley, Bullecourt, May 127-1.

Charles, 2d. Lt. James Arthur Merriman, Shropshire L.I., Rev. James Hamilton Charles, Vicar of Oakham, London, Feb. 10-15.

Chavasse, Capt. Nod Godfrey, V.C., M.C., R.A.M.C., Bishop of Liverpool, Ypres, Aug. 4-17.

Chavasse, Lt. Aidan, King's Liverpool Regt., Bishop of Liverpool, Unknown, France, July 5-17.

Chaytor, Lt. Alban Kingsford, Worcester Regt., Rev. Charles Chator, of St. Helen's, Worcester, Ypres, May 26-15.

Cheales, Clement Bellingham, R.N., Henry John Cheales, Vicar of Friskney, Alexandria, Sep. 5-15.

Chester, Lt. Greville Arthur Bagot, North Staffordshire Regt., Rev, John Greville Chester, Vicar of Gilling, Hazebrouck, Oct. 13-14.

Chester, 2d. Lt. Lewis Charles Bagot, Lancashire Fusiliers, Rev. John Greville Chester, Vicar of Gilling, Ayette, Apr. 5-18.

Chester, Capt. Walter Greville Bagot, M.C., Mentioned in Despatches, Gurkha Rifles, Rev. Algernon Stewart Mackenzie Chester of Ferring, Ramleh, March 28-18.

Cheverton, Lt: Stanley Campbell, Border Regt., Lt.-Col. & Rev. Francis John Cheverton, Vicar of Rowley Regis, Transloy, Jan. 27-17.

Chichester, Capt. Robert Grey, Highland L.I., Rev. Richard Chichester, Rector of Drewsteignton, Ypres, Nov. 13-14.

Chichester, Capt. William George Cubitt, Royal Fusiliers, Rev. Edward Arthur Chichester, Vicar of Dorking, High Wood, Sep. 16-16.

Chilcott, 2d. Lt. Gilbert George Cardew, D. Cornwall's L.I., Rev. W. H. Chilcott of Truro, Kuna, Apr. 18-17.

Cholmondely, Capt. Roger James, M.C., Cheshire Regt. Rev. J. Cholmondely, Onega, Russia, Aug. 14-19.

Christie, 2d. Lt. Cedric P. Pache, Liverpool Regt., Rev. Barry Edwin Christie of Middletown, Armagh, Boulogne, Dec. 14-15.

Christie, Robert Francis Sanderson, Rev. Barry Edwin Christie of Middletown, Armagh, Birmingham, Oct. 15-17,

Christie, 2d. Lt. James Allan, Royal West Surrey, Rev. James Ernest Christie, Vicar of Thornton le Moor, London, Nov. 6-17.

Churchward, Lt. Hubert Allan, Westminster Dragoons, Rev. Marcus Wellesley Churchward of S.P.G., Ypres, Aug. 16-17.

Churchyard, Capt. Arthur Stewart, Rifle Brigade, Rev. Oliver Churchyard, Vicar of St. Matthew's, Newcastle-on-Tyne.

Clapp, 2d. Lt. William Gilbert Elphinstone, Norfolk Yeomanry, Rev. William John Clapp, Rector of Ashley, Arras, Apr. 29-17,

Clapton, 2d. Lt. Arthur, Royal Fusiliers, Rev. Ernest Clapton, Vicar of Hatherdon, Flers, Sept. 15-16.

Clark, Capt. Anthony Dalzell, Sherwood Foresters, Rev., Jaffa, Nov. 25-17.

Clark, Major Gerald Maitland, Northants Regt., Rev. William Maitland Clark, Vicar of Kilmeston, Trones Wood, July 14-16.

Clarke, Arthur Frederick, York and Lancaster Regt., Rev. Alfred Edward Clarke, Vicar of South Leverton, Somme, July 1-16.

Clarke, Lt. Arundel Geoffrey, Rev. A E Clarke, H.M. Oxford Preparatory School.

Clarke, Basil Edward, Canadian E.F., Rev. James Sanderson Clarke, Vicar of Goudhurst, Ypres, Apr. 24-15.

Clarke, Stewart Algernon, The Buffs, Rev. James Sanderson Clarke, Vicar of Goudhurst, Hulluch, Oct. 13-15.

Clarke, Capt. Robert Shuttleworth, Shropshire L.I., Rev. William Shuttleworth Clarke, Vicar of Marstow, Hooge, May 21-15.

Clayton, Lt. Edward Harold, R.A.F., Rev. Arthur Prestwood Clayton, Vicar of Holy Trinity, Ventnor, Valenciennes, Aug. 21-18.

Clesham, Lt. Thomas Henry, Manchester Regt., Rev. Thomas Clesham, Rector of Aasleagh, Galway, Montauban, July 1-15.

Clifford, Lt. Anthony, Dragoon Guards, Rev. Henry William Clifford, C.M.S. Missionary in India, Hooge, June 2-15.

Clinton, Capt. Walter Lawrence, K.R.R.C., Rev. William Osbert Clinton, Rector of Padworth, Belgrade, Nov. 22-18.

Close, Lt. Robert William Mills, Yorkshire Regt., Rev. Arthur Wilfrid Mills Close, Vicar of Hutton Magna, Cramelle, May 27-18.

Coate, 2d. Lt. Alfred Melbourne Coate, R.F.A., Canon Coate, Vicar of Sharnbrook, Mory, Aug. 27-18.

Coate, Capt. William Henry, R. Munster Fusiliers, Canon Coate, Vicar of Sharnbrook, Macedonia, Oct. 26-17.

Cobbold, Lt. Edgar Francis Wanklyn, Cheshire Regt., Rev. Robert Russell Cobbold, Rector of Hitcham, Beauchamp, Jan. 12-16.

Cobbold, Lt. Robert Henry Wanklyn, Rifle Brigade, Rev. Robert Russell Cobbold, Rector of Hitcham, Fleurbaig, Sept. 9-15.

Cobham, Lt. Frederick George Brian, Cambridge Regt., Rev. George Henry Cobham, Rector of Guisborough, Morlancourt, Aug. 8-18.

Cockerill, John, Canadian E.F., Rev James Walter Cockerill, Vicar of Kettlewell, Bailleul, Feb. 20-16.

Cocks, 2d. Lt. Percy Frank Anderson, Queen's West Surrey, Rev. Frank Robert Cocks, Rector of Upton, Basra, May 25-16.

Cocks, Capt. Reginald Somers, M.C., Somerset L.L, Rev. Henry Lawrence Somers Cocks, Rector of Eastnor, Ouderdom, Apr. 24-18.

Codrington, Lt.-Col. Ernest, 120th Rajputs, Rev, Richard Gibson Codrington, C.F., Kut, Apr. 20-16.

Collier, Lt. Frederick Herbert Marse, Lancashire Fusiliers, Rev. Henry Collier, Rector of Holdgate, Arras, Apr. 23 17.

Collins, Lt. John Stratford, Sussex Regt., Rev. J. S. Collins, C.M.S., China, Apr. 5-18.

Collins, 2d. Lt. Neville Lancelot, Sussex Regt., Canon Collins, Rector of Lydd, Pozierre, Aug. 16-16.

Collins, Capt. Percy Plugh Campbell, M.C., York & Lancashire Regt., Canon Collins, Rector of Lydd, Tidworth Military Hospital, Aug. 11-20.

Collinson, Cedric Hasledine, Canadian E.F., Rev. Sydney Garbett Collinson, Vicar of Bradford on Avon, Hill 60, Apr. 26-15.

Collinson, Eric Osmond, Canadian E.F., Rev. Samuel Edward Collinson, Vicar of Broughton, Festubert, May 20-15.

Collisson, 2d. Lt. Evelyn Ernest Arnold, Bedfordshire Regt., Rev. Thomas Collisson, Rector of Gravenhurst, Somme, Feb. 23-16.

Collisson, Frederick Norman, Australian I.F., Rev. Reginald Kingsmill Collisson, Rector of Crafers, South Australia, Ypres, Oct. 1-16.

Colnett, Lt. Richard Daunteshey, Indian Army, Rev. Elson Isaac Colnett, Rector of Willingale Spain, Palestine, Aug. 13-18.

Colquhoun, Major Robert Crosthewaite, R.M.L.I., Rev. Robert Colquhoun, Military Chaplain, India, H.M.S. Invincible, Jutland, May 31-16.

Constable, Major Archibald Thomas, Essex Regt., Rev. Thomas Constable, Vicar of High Hurst Wood, Bethune, Oct. 16-15.

Cooke, Capt. Denys, Black Watch, Canon Cooke of Pitlochry, Givenchy, Apr 18-18.

Cooke, Capt. Hans Hendrick, Connaught Rangers, Rev. Edward Alexander Cooke, Vicar of St. Paul's, Brentford, East Africa, Jan. 24-17.

Cooper, Lt. Corin Henry Benedict, R.E., Rev. Sydney Cooper, Rector of Upper Heyford, Etaples, Nov. 20-16.

Cooper, Lt. Henry Mark Hugh, King Edward's Horse, Rev. July 29-15.

Cooper, 2d. Lt. Horace Burnaby, Wilts Regt., Rev. Horace Rowsell Cooper, Vicar of Thornton, Ovillers, Oct. 23-18.

Copeman, 2d. Lt. Robert George Henry, Essex Regt., Rev. Robert Copeman. Vicar of Everton, Givenchy, Jan. 12-16.

Cordiner, Capt. Roy Grote, M.C., Lincolnshire Regt., Rev. Robert Charles Cordiner, France, Oct. 4-17.

Corfield, Lt. Egerton Anson Frederick, R.F.A., Rev. Egerton Corfield, Rector of Finchamstead, Messines Ridge, June 17-17.

Corfield, 2d. Lt. Hubert Vernon Anchitel, East Lancashire Regt., Rev. Egerton Corfield, Rector of Finchamstead, La Boiselle, July 7-16.

Corke, 2d. Lt. Hubert William, Gloucester Regt., Rev. Hubert Alfred Corke, Vicar of Holy Apostles, Cheltenham, Delville Wood, Sept. 17-16.

Cory, Lt. Edmund Quartermain, Reserve Cavalry, Rev. Robert Frederick Cory, Rector of Higham Gobion, Higham Gobion, Aug. 9-18.

Cory, 2d. Lt. Charles Woolnough, Suffolk Regt., Rev. Charles Page Cory, Rector of Campsea Ashe, Gallipoli, Aug. 12-15.

Cotton, Rev. Robert Hugh Alban, R.A.S.C., Taranto, Oct. 12-18.

Courtenay, Lt. Reginald

Courtney, Lawrence Edward, Royal Fusiliers, Rev. Stanley Thomas Courtney, Vicar of Buffington, Sep. 13-18.

Cowan, Lt. Alan William Russell, Canadian E.F., Rev. Robert David Russell Cowan, Vicar of Bushley, Yprea, Aug. 20-16.

Cowper, 2d. Lt. Leonard Harris, Northumberland Fusiliers, Rev. Herbert William Cowper of Wandsworth, Armentieres, Nov. 7-16.

Cox, Capt. George Pottinger, Essex Regt., Rev. George Innocent Cox, Gallipoli, Dec. 24-15.

Cox, 2d. Lt. Wilfrid Herbert Marshall North, Sherwood Foresters, Rev. Herbert George Charles North Cox, Vicar of Barton on Humber, Newcastle-on-Tyne, March 2-16.

Craven, Rev. George Edward, Chaplain Rifle Brigade, Rev. George Edward Craven, Vicar of Middleton, Salonika, Dec. 7-18.

Crawhall, Lt. Neil Grant, Manchester Regt., Rev. Edward Isaac Laroche Crawhall, Vicar of Ganton, Somme, July 7-16.

Crawhall, 2d. Lt. Fritz Partmore, K.R.R.C., Rev. Edmund Isaac Laroche Crawhall, Vicar of Ganton, Neuve Chapelle, March 10-15.

Cree, Capt. William Cecil Holt, R.F.A., Rev. William Cree of St. Matthias, Earlscourt, Boulogne, Oct. 24-14.

Crick, Capt. Walter Haliburton Routledge, Dorset Regt., Rev. Walter Crick, Vicar of Oving Deir, Ballut, Palestine, Apr. 9-18.

Croft, 2d. Lt. Cyril Talbot Burney, Somerset L.I., Rev. Otho Talbot Bourdois Croft, Rector of South Cadbury, Castle Bromwich, Dec. 8-15.

Crofton, Major Charles Woodward, Worcester Regt., Rev. Henry Woodward Crofton, Chaplain at Rangoon, Gallipoli, Aug. 10-15.

Crofton, Lt. Harold Mowell Manwell, R.N., H.M.S. Curacoa, Rev. Henry Francis Crofton of North Benfleet, Shotley, Nov. 29-18.

Crofts, Capt. Arthur Maughan Humble, R.A.F., Canon Humble Crofts, Rector of Waldron, Dover, Nov. 19-18.

Crofts, Capt. Cyril Mitford Humble, Sussex Regt., Canon Humble Crofts, Rector of Waldron, Richebourg L'Avone, June 30-16.

Croix, Arthur Nicholas de Ste, Royal Sussex Regt., Rev. Henry Miles de Ste Croix, Vicar of St. Saviour's Guernsey, Halluch, Oct. 20-15.

Crompton, 2d. Lt. Thomas Sherwood, Border Regt., Rev. William Henry Crompton, Vicar of Shap, Windermere, Oct. 29-15.

Crompton, 2d. Lt. Arthur Harold, Border Regt., Rev. William Henry Crompton, Vicar of Shap, Somme, July 3-16.

Crookham, Lt. Hugh Anthony Rupert, Cambridge Regt., Canon Crookham, Vicar of Wisbech, Houplines, Aug. 3-15.

Cropper, 2d. Lt. Alexander, Wilts Regt., Rev. Charles Henry Edward Cropper, Vicar of Holy Trinity, Clifton, Albert, Oct. 22-16.

Cropper, Capt. Edward Percival, M. C., Croix de Guerre, West Yorkshire Regt., Rev. James Cropper, Rector of Wombwell, Kuna, March 25-18,

Crosby, 2d. Lt. John Claud Parry, King's Liverpool Regt., Rev. John Hawke Crosby of Ely, Houplines, Jan. 21-18.

Crosse, Lt. Robert Grant, West Kent Regt., Rev. Thomas George Crosse, Rector of Ickham, Fricourt, July 14-16.

Crosse, Capt. Thomas Latimer, Border Regt., Rev. Thomas George Crosse, Rector of Ickham, Maricourt, July 3-16.

Grossman, 2d. Lt. Guy Danvers Mainwaring, Welsh Regt., Rev. Charles Danvers Crossman, Rector of High Ham, Mametz, July 10-16.

Crowley, 2d. Lt. Cedric Hugh, Warwickshire Regt., Rev. Cedric Edwin Crowley, Rector of Chilbolton, St. Julien, Apr. 25-15.

Crowley, Lt. Philip, Royal Lancasters, Rev. Henry Ernest Crowley, Rector of Albury, Cambria, July 7-17.

Crozier, 2d. Lt. James Cyril Baptist, Munster Fusiliers, Rev. Henry Wilcocks Crozier, Vicar of St. Matthias, Stockport, Streuse, Aug. 27-14.

Cruddas, 2d. Lt. Sandwith George Peter, Duke of Cornwall's L.I., Rev. William Sandwith Cruddas, Rector of Withiel, Ypres, Sept. 21-15.

Cullen, 2d. Lt. Gerald Somerville Yeats, Royal Irish Fusiliers, Rev. James Edward Cullen of Ballyheigue, Kerry, Apr. 11-17.

Cullwick, Henry Palmer, Australian I.F., Canon Cullwick, Vicar of Takapau, N.Z., Melbourne, Aug. 15-18.

Culshaw, 2d. Lt. Ronald Henry, West Yorkshire Regt., Rev. George Harold Culshaw, Rector of Iver Heath, Meule, July 14-18.

Cummins, Capt. Herbert Charles Bruce, Seaforth Highlanders, Rev. W. H. Cummins, Nieppe, May 7-16.

Cure, Capt. Basil Alfred Capel, Gloucester Regt., Rev. Edward Capel Cure, Rector of Stower Provost, Lahana, Greece, Oct. 1-16.

Curties, Capt. Lionel Charles Alfred, Machine Gun Corps. Rev. Thomas Arthur Curties, Vicar of St. Michael's, Wakefield, Hulluch, Sept. 26-15.

Darling, Lt. William Oliver Fortescue, Royal Irish Rifles, Rev. Oliver Warner Darling, Rector of Killesk, Co. Wexford, Bois Grenier, Oct. 19-15.

Darling, 2d. Lt. Claud Henry Whish, Royal Irish Rifles, Rev. Oliver Warner Darling, Rector of Killesk, Co. Wexford, Le Touquet, Dec. 12-15.

Darnell, Major Aubrey Hugh, D.S.O., Australian I.F., Rev. Francis Aubrey Darnell, C.F., Roisel, Sept. 24-18.

Dashwood, Major Claud Burrard Lewes, Northumberland Fusiliers, Rev. Robert Lewes Dashwood, Rector of Stanford on Soar, Bailleul, Apr. 26-16.

Davenport, 2d. Lt. Francis Edward Alexander Orme, K. Shropshire L.I., Rev. Edward Davenport, Rector of Draughton, Langincourt, March 21-18.

Davies, Lt. Arthur Gwynne Hughes, M.C., Royal Welsh Fusiliers, Rev. Thomas Hughes Davies, Vicar of Bettws Cedewain, Palestine, Sept. 21-18.

Davies, Lt. David Ethelston, Royal Welsh Fusiliers, Rev. John Davies, Rector of Llangybi, Cambrai, June 18-17.

Davies, Geoffrey Frangeon, H.A.C., Rev. Frangeon Davies, Locre, May 10-15.

Davies, Lt. George Herbert, Shropshire L.I., Rev. John Bayley Davies, Rector of Waters Upton, Hooge, Aug. 10-15.

Davies, Lt. Jack Tyssul, R.N.R., Rev. Daniel Sawelian Davies, Rector of Kilrhedyn, Chatham, Jan. 20-17.

Davies, Lt. Ivan Beauclerk Hart, R.A.F., Rev. John Hart Davies, Rector of Northolt, July 27-17.

Davies, Lt. Kenneth George, R.E., Rev. Wilfred Harold Davis, Rector of St. George's in the Fields, Vimy, May 19-17.

Davies, Roderick Simpson Llewelyn, Worcester Yeomanry Rev. David Llewelyn Davies, Vicar of Little Dewchurch, Oct. 29-17.

Davies, 2d. Lt. Walter Llewelyn, Shropshire L.I., Rev. John Bayley Davies, Rector of Waters Upton, Corbie, July 18-17.

Davis, Harold Pashley, Somerset L.I., Rev. Edward Davis, Vicar of Chevithorne, Havrincourt Wood, Sept. 11-18.

Davis, Bernard Cantrell, N.Z.E.F., Rev. Henry John Davis, Vicar of Hampden, N.Z., Passchendale, Oct. 2-17.

Davis, Eric Nathaniel, Sergeant N.Z.E.F., Rev. Henry John Davis, Vicar of Hampden, N.Z., France, Apr. 5-18.

Davis, Lt. Ronald H., R.A.F.

Day, Lt. Geoffrey Reynolds, Bedfordshire Regt., Fellow of Emmanuel College, Cambridge, Rev. Archibald Day, Vicar of Malvern Link, France, Aug. 27-16.

Day, 2d. Lt. Herbert, Loyal North Lancashire Fusiliers, Rev. Benjamin William Day, Rector of St. Peter's, Sandwich, Boiselle, July 10-16.

Day, 2d. Lt. Maurice, R. Bucks Regt., Rev. Benjamin William Day, Rector of St. Peter's Sandwich, Fromelles, May 9-15.,

Day, Capt. John Edward, Royal Irish Regt., Dean of Waterford, Bailleul, Apr. 6-17.

Day, 2d. Lt. Maurice Charles, 13th Rajputs, Dean of Waterford, Tanga, East Arfica, Nov. 3-14.

Dean, Lt. G W W Denman, R.M.L.I., Rev. Richard Denman Dean, Rector of Woodbridge.

Dean, Lt. Leonard Widlake, N.Z.E.F., Rev. Oliver Dean, Vicar of S. Andrew's, Napier, N.Z., Bapaume, Sept. 3-18.

Deane, Bernard Reginald John, New Zealand E.F., Rev. John Deane, Vicar of Isle Brewers, Gallipoli, Aug. 28-15.

Deane, Edmund Bonar, Canadian E.F., Rev. Charles Henry Deane, Vicar of Willoughby, Ypres, June 3-16.

Dearmer, Lt. Christopher, R.N.V.R., Rev. Percy Dearmer, Vicar of St. Mary's, Hampstead, Gallipoli, Oct. 6-15.

Debenham, Lt. Herbert, East Lancashire Regt., Rev. John Wilmott Debenham, Gallipoli, Aug. 9-15.

Deed, Capt. John Cyril, R.M.L.I., Rev. John George Deed, Vicar of Nuneaton, H.M.S. Formidable, Jan. 1-15.

Deedes, Capt. Herbert Philip, K.R.R.C., Rev. Phillip Deedes, Rector of Little Parndon, Albert, July 15-16.

Denne, Major William Henry, D.S.O., Bedfordshire Regt., Rev. Richard Henry Denne, Rector of Brimsfield, London, Feb. 21-17.

Delap, 2d. Lt. John Follamsbee Bredin, Yorkshire Regt., Rev. Louis Bredin Delap, Vicar of Benhall, Oct. 18-16.

Denny, 2d. Lt. Barry Maynard Rynd, Liverpool Regt., Rev. Edward Denny, Vicar of St. Peter's, Vauxhall, Ypres, Oct. 26-14.

Derrick, Capt. John Leslie, East Yorkshire Regt., Rev. John George Derrick, Ypres, Aug. 27-17.

Devas, Lt. Arthur, Essex Regt., Rev. A C Devas, Vicar of St. Peter's, Devizes, Feb. 15-16.

Dew, Capt. Walter Frederick, Bedford Regt., Rev. Henry Dew, Vicar of Whitney, Drewsteignton, July 3-15.

Dewar, Lt. David, M.G.C., Mentioned in Despatches, Rev. David Dewar, Vicar of Holy Trinity, Loughborough, Jussy March 22-18

Dewar, 2d. Lt. Lancelot John Austin, R.M.L.I. Rev. David Dewar, Vicar of Holy Trinity, Loughborough Beaumont Hamel, Nov. 13-16,

Dewing, Lt.-Col. Robert Edward, D.S.O., Mentioned in Despatches, Berkshire Regt., Rev. Richard Standly Dewing, Vicar of Badwell Ash, Apr. 4-18.

Dickenson, Lt. Aubrey Greville Newton, K.R.R.C., Rev. Lenthall Greville Dickenson, D.S.O., Vicar of Downton, July 1-16.

Dickenson, Lt. Lawrence Aubrey Finnes Wingfield, Bedfordshire Regt., Rev. Francis Wingfield Dickenson, Rector of Inworth, Ypres, May 10-15.

Digby, Rev. Lionel Kenelm, Norfolk Regt., Rector of Tittleshall, Fancourt, Oct. 18-18.

Dingle, Capt. Arthur James, East Yorkshire Regt., Rev. Arthur Trehane Dingle, Rector of Eaglescliffe, Gallipoli, Aug. 22-15.

Dingle, Hugh John Surgeon, R.N.V.A., Rev. Arthur Trehane Dingle, Rector of Eaglescliffe, H.M.S. Petard, Jutland, May 31-16.

Dixon, 2d. Lt. Carl Penrose, R.A.F., Rev. Charles Ernest Dixon, Vicar of St. George's Barnsley, Mendinghem, Oct. 25-17.

Dodgson, Lt. Kenneth Vernon, Devonshire Regt., Rev. Francis Vivian Dodgson, Vicar of Ellacombe, Loos, Sept. 25-15.

Doddrell, 2d. Lt. Kenneth Curling, Wilts. Regt., Rev. Curling Finzel Doddrell, Rector of English Bicknor, Sept. 19-18.

Dominey, George William, Scots Guards, Rev. George William Dominey, Rector of St. Vincent's, Edinburgh, Armentieres, Dec. 18-14,

Donkin, Rev. Arthur Donkin, Rector of Semer.

Donnell, 2d. Lt. Arthur Patrick, Northumberland Fusiliers, R.A.F., Rev. Charles Ernest Havelock Donnell, Vicar of Stamfordham, Norfolk, Dec. 4-16.

Donnell, Lt. Ernest Tudor, R.N., Rev. Charles Ernest Havelock Donnell, Vicar of Stamfordham, H.M.S. Shark, Jutland, May 31-16.

Donovan, Sub-Lt. Edgar Claude, R.N.V.R., Rev. Alexander Donovan, Vicar of Garton, Belgium, Apr. 26-17.

Dowding, Capt. C. G. M.C., Punjabis, Rev. William Berkeley Dowding, C.F., Nov. 11-17.

Dowding, Midshipman Geoffrey Marischal, R.N., Rev. Charles Dowding, Rector of Tichborne, Coronel, H.M.S. Good Hope, Nov. 1-14.

Downman, Lt. Bernard Vincent Ridout, Sherwood Foresters, Rev. Frank Percival Downman of Horfield, Somme, Sept. 21-16.

Dowse, Lt. Charles Edward, Dublin Fusiliers, Chancellor Dowse, Rector of Monkstown, Co. Dublin, Gallipoli, Aug. 16-15.

Dowse, Lt. Henry Harvey, R.A.F., Chancellor Dowse, Rector of Monkstown, Co. Dublin, Genoa Hospital, Nov. 10-18.

Dowse, Capt. Robert Joseph Gordon, A.S.C., Dean of Connor, Douai, Dec. 19-18.

Doyne, Lt. Philip Denys, Oxford & Bucks L.I., Rev. Philip Valentine Doyne, Vicar of Headington Quarry, Dec. 29-15.

Drake, Capt. Robert Edward, Lincolnshire Regt., Rev. John Drake, Rector of Wratting, Maine, Sept. 8-14.

Draper, William P. B., Shropshire L.I., The Master of the Temple.

Drought, Capt. Charles Frederick, Lincolnshire Regt., Canon Drought of Toorak, Melbourne, Le Touquet, Dec. 31-15.

Drought, Major George Thomas Acton, R.F.A., Rev. George M. Drought, Newtownmount Kennedy, Co. Wicklow, June 15-15.

Dudley, Capt. David, 91st Punjabis, Rev. Francis Dudley, Vicar of Overmonnow, Neuve Chapelle, May 9-15.

Dugdale, Rev. Richard Williams C.F., M.C., R.A.F., Rev. Sydney Dugdale, Rector of Whitchurch, Salop, Caudry, Oct. 23-18.

Duncan, 2d. Lt. Kenneth William Allan, Liverpool Regt., Rev. George Allan Duncan, Vicar of Weston Point, Harduil, May 9-18.

Dunn, 2d. Lt. Ralph Ellis, Somerset L.I., Rev. Henry Ellis Dunn, Vicar of Upton, Somme, July 1-16.

Durand, Capt. Francis William, Munster Fusiliers, Rev. Havilland Durand, Vicar of Earley, Givenchy, Dec. 22-14.

Durand, Rev. Havilland Montague, Australian I.F., Rev. Havilland Durand, Vicar of Earley, Gallipoli, Apr. 25-15.

Durant, Lt. Norman, Gloucester Regt., Rev. W. F. Durant, March 12-16.

Durrant, Midshipman Humphrey Mercer Lancelot, R.N., Rev. Charles Aubrey Durrant, Vicar of Wetherby, H.M.S. Hapshire, June 6-16.

Duxbury, 2d Lt. Herbert Cecil, R.A.F., Rev. Anyon Herbert Duxbury, Vicar of St. Mary Magdalene, Southwark, Cambria, May 11-17.

Dyson, Cecil Venn, Malay States Volunteers, Rev. Samuel Dyson of Koilash, Singapore, Feb. 15-15.

Eagles, Major Charles Edward Campbell, D.S.O., R.M.L.I., Canon Eagles, Vicar of Coughton, H.M.S. Iris, Apr. 23-18.

Eales, Lt. Charles Wilfred, Devon Regt., Rev. Henry William Eales, Vicar of Lewannick, Sept. 27-18.

Eddis, Lt.-Com. Christopher John Francis, R.N., Croix de Guerre, Rev. John Elwin Eddis, Vicar of Holy Trinity, Ryde, H.M.S. Scimitar, Scapa Flow, Oct. 15-18.

Edgell, Lt. Richard Fayrer Arnold, Scottish Borderers, Rev. Richard Arnold Edgell, Rector of Beckley, Hill 60, May 5-15.

Edmunds, Capt. Charles Vincent, Essex Regt., Rev. Charles Edmunds, Vicar of Broomfield, Gaza, March, 26-17.

Edwards, Lt. Hard Willis, East Lancashire Regt., Rev. Harri Edwards, Perronne, Apr. 28-17.

Edwards, Lt. Henry H. Laidley Garland, Welsh Fusiliers, Archbishop of Wales, Festubert, May 16-15.

Edwards, Capt. Llewelyn Albert, Warwickshire Regt., Rev. Jeremiah John Edwards, Vicar of Berrow, Germaine, March 23-18.

Edwardes, Lt. Thomas, York & Lancaster Regt., Rev. George Edwardes, Vicar of St. John's, Toxeth Park, Liverpool, Apr. 12-18.

Egerton, 2d. Lt. Arthur Oswald, Shropshire L.I., Prebendary Egerton, of Lichfield, Loos, Sept. 25-15.

Elans, 2d. Lt. Willingham Richard, East Yorkshire Regt., Rev. George Richard Ekins, Vicar of St. Timothy, Sheffield, Oppy Wood, May 3-17.

Ekins, Lt. Franklin George, Royal Irish, M.C., with bar, St. George's Cross, Rev. George Richard Ekins, Vicar of St. Timothy, Sheffield, Cherbourg, Jan. 27-19.

Ellershaw, Brig.-General Wilfrid, Ld. Kitchener's Staff, Rev. J. Ellershaw, Rector of Chewstoke, Hampshire, June 5-16.

Elliott, Angelus Basil, Australian I.F., Rev. Robert Elliott, Rector of Queanbeyan, N.S.W., Pozieres, July 26-16.

Elliott, 2d. Charles Arthur Boileau, Somerset L.I., Rev. Charles Lister Boileau Elliott, Rector of Tattingstone, Aubigny, Apr. 12-17.

Elliott, Capt. Francis, Reserve of Officers, Canon Elliott, Vicar of North Carlton, Jubaland, Feb. 2-16.

Ellis, Capt. Francis Bevis, Northumberland Fusiliers, Hon. and Rev. Canon Ellis, Rector of Morpeth, Sept. 26-16.

Ellis, Lt. Basil Herbert, Shropshire L.I., Rev. Henry Maitland Ellis, Vicar of Hedge End, Hooge, June 15-15.

Ellis, Lt. Yvo Lempriere, Hampshire Regt., Rev. Henry Maitland Ellis, Vicar of Hedge End, Cambrai, May 29-16.

Ellis, 2d. Lt. Hughie Lodwick Maldwyn, Welsh Fusiliers, Rev. Evan Lodwick Ellis, Rector of Ysceifiog, Bullecourt, May 5-17.

Ellis, Capt. Stanley Venn, R.N., Rev. Henry' Venn Ellis, Rector of Alderton, H.M.S. Defence, Jutland, May 31-16.

Ellwood, Lt. Geoffrey Thomas Levick, Leicester Regt., Rev. Charles Edward Ellwood, Rector of Cottesmore, Bazentin, July 14-16.

Elphick, Harold Samuel, Wilts Regt., Rev. James Strudwick Elphick, Vicar of St Mark's, Forest Gate, Acheux, Aug. 25-18.

Elphick, Leslie Strudwick, Royal Warwickshire Regt., Rev. James Strudwick Elphick, Vicar of St. Mark's, Forest Gate, Poperinghe, May 8-18.

Elstob, Lt.-Col. Wilfrith, Manchester Regt., V.C., D.S.O., M.C., Canon Elstob, Vicar of Capesthorne, Manchester Hill, St. Quentin, March 21-18.

Elton, 2d. Lt. George Kenward, Hants Regt., Rev. George Goudenough Elton, Vicar of Nether Wallop, Guidecourt, Oct. 18-16.

Elwin, 2d. Lt. Frank Harold, Wilts. Regt., March 14-15.

Emmet, Capt. Frederick Herbert, Leicestershire Regt., Rev. William Edward Emmet, Vicar of Whaddon, Bezentin, July 14-16.

English, George William, Canadian E.F., Rev. William Henry English, Rector of Paynton Sask, Canada, Ypres, Apr. 24-15.

Eppstein, Lt. William Wallace, R.N.A.S., Rev. Dr. William Charles Eppstein, Rector of Lambourne, Zeebrugge, May 12-17.

Escott, Lt. Murray Robertson Sweet, Liverpool Regt., Rev. Edward Herbert Sweet Escott, of Dulwich College, Missy, Sept. 20-14.

Ethell, 2d. Lt. John Oliver, Australian I.F., Rev. Alfred William Ethell, Rector of Laidley, Queensland, Zonnebeke, Oct. 4-17.

Evans, Lt. Alexander Easson, Canadian E. F., Rev. Maurice John Evans, Festubert, Jan 5-16.

Evans, Lt. Frank Graham, Royal Welsh Fusiliers, Rev. David Williams Evans, Vicar of Llanrhaiadr, Fagairchely, Sept. 25-16.

Evans, Herbert Walton, Australian I.F., Archdeacon of St. Asaph, Amiens, July 16-18.

Evans, Capt. Llewellyn Lewis Meredith, R.A.F., Rev. John Lewis Evans, Vicar of Ford End, English Channel, May 9-19.

Evans, 2d. Lt. Neville Vernon, South Wales Borderers, Rev. John David Evans, Vicar of Treherbert, Langemarck, Aug. 16-17.

Evans, Samuel John, Royal Welsh Fusiliers, Rev. William Evans, Vicar of Tregaer, Loos, Sept. 25-15.

Everett, John Eric Murray, East Kent Mounted Rifles, Rev. Frederick John Everett, Vicar of Aylesford, Gallipoli, Oct. -15.

Evill, Capt. Christopher Percy, M.C., R.E., Rev. Henry Marten Evill, Vicar of St. Martin's, Hereford, Meerut, July 17-18.

Ewbank, Capt. John Walter, M.C., Border Regt., Rev. John Ewbank, Rector of Bolton, Cambrai, Nov. 30-17.

Ewbank, 2d. Lt. Leonard, Border Regt., Rev. John Ewbank, Rector of Bolton, Ypres, Feb. 23-16.

Eykin, Capt. Gilbert Davidson Pitt, Royal Scots, Rev. Pitt Eykin, Vicar of Magor, St, Julien, Apr. 24-15.

Faithfull, 2d. Lt. Francis William Alexander, Seaforth Highlanders, Rev. Robert Colquhoun Faithfull, Rector of Peakirk, Ypres, July 4-15.

Falkner, Capt. Arthur Newstead, L. N. Lancashire Regt., Rev. Robert Henry Falkner, Rector of Woodham Walter, Rouen, July 20-16.

Fallowes, Lt. John Tyrel Champion, Suffolk Regt., Rev. John Prince Fallowes, Rector of Heene, Somme, Sept. 15-16.

Farmar, Lt. Henry Charles Maclean, K.R.R.C., Rev. James Edmund Gamul Farmar, Rector of Waddesden, Ypres, May 10-15.

Farquhar, 2d. Lt. Ronald George, Royal Warwickshire Regt., Rev. John Henry Farquhar, Rector of Silvington, Mesopotamia, March 29-17.

Farquharson, Capt. Lewis Shaw, Royal Scots, Rev. James Alexander Farquharson of Spital, Ypres, May 12-15.

Farrar, 2d. Lt. Ernest Bristowe, Devons, Rev. Charles Druce Farrar, Vicar of Micklefield, Roussoy, Sept. 18-18.

Farrar, 2d. Lt. Herbert Ronald, Leicester Regt., Rev. Herbert William Farrar, Rector of Barcombe, Wolverghem, Dec. 24-14.

Farrer, Major Henry Wyndham Francis Blackburne, M.C. 2 bars, Croix de Guerre, 1914 Star, R.F.A., Canon Farrar of Sarum, Mazinghim, Oct. 30-18

Featherstone, 2d. Lt. George Herbert, Yorkshire L.I., Rev. Ralph John Featherstone, Vicar of St. Luke, Thornaby, Somme, July 1-16.

Feetham, Maj.-General Edward, 39th Division, Rev. William Feetham, Vicar of Penrhos, Demoin, Nov. 29-18.

Felton, 2d. Lt. Hubert Ratcliffe, Worcester Regt., Rev. Walter Felton, Vicar of St. Johns, Walsall, Ypres, Oct. 9-17.

Fendall, Frederick Selwyn, N.Z.E.F., Rev. Frederick Philip Fendall, Vicar of Glenmark, N.Z., Drokenhurst, Dec. 8-16.

Fenton, Major Bede Liddell, Dorset Regt., Rev. Enos Fenton, Vicar of Shotton, July 15-17.

Ferguson, Lt. Duncan Macintyre Grant, K.O. Scottish Borderers, Rev. John Grant Ferguson, of Innerlethen, Boulogne, May 14-15.

Ferguson, Capt Donald Francis, Scottish Horse, Rev. Edwin Augustus Ferguson, Rector of Milton, Bullecourt, May 7-17.

Ffrench, 2d. Lt. George Edward, R.A.F., Rev. Lebel Holbrooke Edward Ffrench, Incumbent of Kilconnell, Galway, Pemes, May 23-18.

Field, 2d. Lt. Charles Cecil, West Kent Regt., Rev. Walter St. John Field, Vicar of Fordcombe, St. Eloi, March 30-16.

Filleul, Lt. Leonard Amauri, Somerset L.I., Rev. Phillip William Girdlestone Filleul, Rector of Alford, St. Julien, Oct 21-14.

Finch, Lt.-Col. Herbert Marshall, Berkshire Regt., Rev. Thomas Ross Finch, of Penwortham, Preston, Fromelles, May 9-15.

Firminger, 2d. Lt. Thomas, The Buffs, Rev. Thomas David Charles Firminger, Vicar of Charlton Adam, Somme, Sept. 3-16.

Fischer, Lt. Walde Gerard, Australian I.F., Rev. Carl Hermann Fischer, Vicar of Redcliffe, Queensland, Somme, Apr. 5-18.

Fishboume, Capt. Charles Eustace, R.E., Rev. Edward Alexander Fishbourne, Rector of Gresford, Chatham, June 10-15.

Fisher, Capt. Harold, D.S.O., Manchester Regt., Canon Fisher of Hemel Hempstead, Le Bassee, Dec. 16-14.

Fisher, Kenneth Cuthbert Brown, Duke of Wellington's Regt., Rev. John Brown Fisher, Vicar of Muston, Fonquivillers, Nov. 3-16.

Fisher, Thomas Wilfrid, Border Regt., Rev. Arthur Thomas Fisher, Vicar of Pocklington, Balkans, Feb. 21-17.

Fitzpatrick, Capt. Thomas Gordon, Royal Irish Fusiliers, Rev. William Fitzpatrick, Rector of Dysart, Somme, Sept. 16-16.

Fitzpatrick, Lt. Wilfrid, Canadian E.F., Rev. Henry Fitzpatrick, Chaplain of St. George's, Hyderabad, Ypres, Apr. 24-15.

Fleming, Lt.-Col. Laurence Julius Le, East Surrey Regt., Rev. John Le Fleming, of Tonbridge, France, March 21-18.

Fletcher, 2d. Lt. Noel William Scott, Durham L.I., Canon Fletcher, Rector of St. Matthew's, Ipswich, Norval, March 7-17.

Fleury, Hugo Valentine, New Zealand E.F., Rev. Louis Richard Fleury, Rector of Kilworth, Cork, Loos, Sep. 8-17.

Fleury, John Charles, New Zealand E.F., Rev. Louis Richard Fleury, Rector of Kilworth, Cork, Flers, Oct. 3-16.

Fleury, Leopold M'Clintock, R.N., Rev. Louis Richard Fleury, Rector of Kilworth, Cork, Gallipoli, May, 6-15.

Flory, Arnold Augustus, R.N., Rev. Henry William Flory, Vicar of St. Matthew's, Littleport, Liverpool, Sept. 28-18.

Flory, 2d. Lt. Perceval James, Bedford Regt., Rev. William Henry Flory, Vicar of St. Matthew's, Littleport, Arras, Aug. 22-18.

Flory, 2d. Lt. William Henry, Oxford & Bucks L.I., Rev. William Henry Flory, Vicar of St. Matthew's, Littleport, St. Quentin, March 21-18.

Flowers, Capt. Humphrey French, R.A.F., Rev. John French Flowers, Vicar of Gt. Carlton, Camrai. Oct. 14-18.

Flowers, Lt. William Henry Field, York & Lancaster Regt., Rev. John French Flowers, Vicar of Gt. Carlton, Mont de Lille, Apr. 15-18.

Floyd, Guy Tyrwhitt, Canadian E.F., Rev. George Floyd, Rector of Frilsham, Vimy Ridge, May 5-17.

Fontaine, Lt. Edward Harold De, London Regt., Rev. Alfred Hutchings De Fontaine, Rector of Bletchingley, Le Treport, Nov, 17-15.

Foote, Major Trevor Mawdsley, North Lancashire Regt., Rev. Lundy Edward William Foote, Vicar of St. Peter's, Harrogate, Ypres, July 10-14.

Ford, Capt. Francis William, M.C., Cambridge Regt., Rev. John Thomas Ford, Rector of Rede, Menin, Sept. 26-17.

Ford, Lt. Kenneth George Haslam, Cheshire Regt., Rev. George Adam Ford, Rector of Ashill, Archdeacon of Lucknow, Ploeg-street, Nov. 30-15.

Forde, Lt. Kenneth Rowley, East Kent Regt., Canon Forde, Rector of Tamlaghtfralagan, Londonderry, Ypres, July 23-15.

Forneri, David Alwyn Forneri, Canadian E.F., Canon Richard Sykes Forneri, Rector of St. Luke's, Kingston, Ontario, Vimy Ridge, March 1-17.

Forrest, 2d. Lt. Austin Lancelot, K.R.R.C., Canon Forrest, Vicar of Pemberton, Guillemont, Sept. 3-16.

Forrest, 2d. Lt. Laurence Bernard, K.R.R.C., Canon Forrest, Vicar of Pemberton, Arras, May 20-17.

Forster, Lt. Christopher Jack, R.A.F., Rev. Francis Samuel Forster, Vicar of Frindsbury, Ypres, July 21-17.

Fosbrooke, 2d. Lt. Cuthbert, Durham L.I., Rev. Arthur Middleton Fosbrooke, Vicar of Hartshill, Ypres, July 19-17.

Foster, 2d. Lt. Herbert Knollys, Gloucester Regt., Rev. Herbert Charles Foster, Canon of Gloucester, Gheluvelt, Oct 29-14.

Foster, Lt. Lawrence Talbot Lisle, Durham L.I., Rev. Albert John Foster, Vicar of Wooton, Gallipoli, Aug. 7-15.

Fothergill, Cuthbert Richard Page, Canadian E.F., Rev. Rowland John Fothergill, Rector of Drummondville, Canada, St. Julien, Apr. 24-15.

Fox. 2d. Lt. Goeffrey Noel Storrs, West Yorks, Rev. Noel Storrs Fox, Rector of Holy Trinity, York, Caix, March 28-18.

Fox, Lt. Lawrence Anselm Storrs, West Yorks, Rev. Edwin Sotrrs Fox, Vicar of Hawkser, Wimereux, Apr. 27-18.

Fox, Lt. Thomas Noel, Somerset L.I., Rev. James Charles Fox, Rector of Temple Coombe, Rustchurch, Dec. 12-18.

Foxell, Capt. Edward William Lanchester, The Buffs, Rev. William James Foxell, Rector of St. Swithin's, London, June 11-17.

Foyster, Capt. Philip Tillard, R.E., Rev. George Alfred Foyster, Rector of All Saints, Hastings, Le Touquet, Dec.11-16.

Frampton, Waltr John, Australian I.F., Rev. James Frampton, of Ascot, Alexandria, May 5-15.

Francis, Gilbert Bryan, New Zealand E.F., Rev. David Francis, Vicar of Liandygwydd, Malta, Nov. 13-15.

Frayling, 2d. Lt. Michael Stapleton, R.F.A., Rev. Edwin John Frayling, Vicar of Harwich, Flers, Sept. 16-10.

Freeman, 2d. Lt. John Bentley, West Kent Regt., Rev. Herbert Bentley Freeman, Vicar of Burton on Trent, Manin, Sept. 20-17.

Frend, 2d. Lt. Hugh Palliser, Northants Regt., Rev. John Palliser, Rector of Collingtree, St. Leger, March 20-17.

Fuller, Capt. John Severn, R.F.A., Rev. Richard Henry Fuller, Rector of Emmanuel, Loughborough, Hongkong, March 15-19.

Furley, Edward Hugh Mainwaring, East African Mounted Rifles, Rev. Edward Mainwaring Furley, of Pontesbury, Ingido, Nov. 3-14.

Furley, 2d. Lt. George Frederick, Canadian E.F., Rev. Henry Furley, Rector of Kingsworth, Poperinghe, Nov. 8-17.

Furley, 2d. Lt. Robert Basil, Oxford &Bucks L.I., Rev. Henry Furley, Rector of Kingsnorth, France, Jan. 25-16.

Fureaux, Lt. Philip Templer, Liverpool Regt., Rev. Walter Coppleston Furneaux, Vicar of Dean, Kimboltoa, Hunts., Ypres, Oct. 26-14.

Fyldes, 2d. Lt. Aubrey William, E. Lancashire Regt., Rev. William Fyldes, Vicar of Witton, Gallipoli, Aug. 9-15.

Fyson, Lt. Geoffry, Royal Scots, Bishop Fyson of Hokkaido, Japan, Rector of Elmley Lovett, Salonika, Sept. 4-18.

Fyson Oliver, Canadian E.F., Bishop Fyson of Hokkaido, Rector of Elmley Lovett, Langemarck, Apr. 23-15.

Gabell, 2d. Lt. Douglas Ridley Clunes, R.A.F., Rev. Arthur Charles Gabell, Rector of Swindon, Chippenham, July 12-18.

Gallwey, Lt. Philip Francis Payne, 21st Lancers, Rev. Francis Henry Payne Gallwey, Rector of Sessay, Messines, Oct, 31-14.

Garnett, Capt. Claude Lionel, R.G.A., Canon Garnett, of Chester, Rector of Thetford, Kut, Dec. 31-15.

Garnier, Capt. John Warreen, West Surrey Regt., Canon Garnier, of Norwich, London, Nov. 28-15.

Gardner, Lt. Cyril Gower, Grenadier Guards, Rev. Frederick Thomas Gardner, Rector of Goldhanger, Les Boeufs Sep. 15-16.

Gaskell, Capt. John Charles Temple, 69th Punjabis, Rev. Thomas Kynaston Gaskell, Rector of Longthorpe, East Africa, Aug. 5-17.

Gaster, 2d. Lt. Percy Stuart, R.A.F., Rev. Percy Gaster, Vicar of St. Paul's, Greenwich, Montrose, Apr. 21-18.

Gaussen, Lt. David Newbould, Bedfordshire Regt., Rev. Charles Edward Gaussen, Vicar of Nettleden, Delville Wood, July 31-16.

Gedge, Joseph Theodore, Staff Paymaster, R.N., He was the first British officer to lose his life in the War, Rev. Edmund Gedge, Vicar of Marden, H.M.S. Amphion, Aug. 16-14.

Gedge, Lt. Peter, Suffolk Regt., Rev. Edmund Gedge, Vicar of Marden, Hulluch, Oct. 13-15.

Gee, Capt. Reginald Claude Moline, M.C., Rev. Claude Valentine Gee, Vicar of Castletown, Nov. 7-18.

Gell, 2d. Lt. Christopher Stowell, West Yorkshire Regt., Canon Gell, of York, Vicar of Holme, Somme, Sep. 18-16.

Gepp, Capt. Nicholas Melvill, Yorkshire L.I., Rev. Nicholas Parker Gepp, Canon of Ely, Rector of Witchingham, Aug. 6-15.

Gibbs, Lt. Col. William Beresford, Worcester Regt., Rev. William Cobham Gibbs, Rector of Clyst St. George, Thiepval, Sep. 3-16.

Gibbs, Rev. Edward Reginald, C.F., Grenadier Guards, Rev. William Cobham Gibbs, Rector of Clyst St. George, Boisleaux, March 29-18.

Gibson, Lt. McKenzie, N.Z.E.F., Rev. McKenzie Gibson, Chaplain N.Z.E.F., Paschendale, Oct. 12-17.

Gibson, Lt. Pendarves Christopher Foil, Royal Fusiliers, Rev. Edward Pendarves Gibson, Rector of Stock, Monchy, Apr. 10-17.

Gibson, Lt. Robert Bowness, South Stafford Regt., Rev. Thomas William Gibson, Rector of Cranham, Troones Wood, July 11-16.

Gilbanks, Lt. Richard Parker, Border Regt., Rev. William Foster Gilbanks, Rector of Gt. Orton, Gallipoli, Aug. 9-15.

Gillett, Capt. George Maurice Gerald, Leicester Regt., Rev. Hugh Hodgson Gillett, Rector of Compton, Somme, Sep. 26-16.

Girling, Capt. Theodore Augustus, Canadian E.F., Mentioned in Despatches, Rev. William Henry Girling, Vicar of Wilshaw, Namur, March 1-19.

Given, Capt. Maurice, M.M., Sherwood Foresters, Rev. James Given, Vicar of Chapel en le Frith, Denain, May 17-18.

Glanville, Major Hugh Fanshawe, R.A.F., Mentioned in Despatches, Rev. Owen Fanshawe Glanville of South Brent, Scotland, May 25-18.

Gleave, John Howard Newberry, Canadian E.F., Rev. Thomas Gleave, Vicar of Douglas, Mt. Kemmel, Sep. 1-16.

Glossop, 2d. Lt. Ernest Edward, Somerset L.I., Canon Glossop, of St. Alban's, Bailleul, May 2-15.

Godfrey, Edward Baker, Canadian E.F., Rev. George Godfrey, Vicar of Redbourne, Loos, July 27-17.

Goodall, Capt. Marcus Herbert, York & Lancaster, Canon Goodall, Vicar of Rotherham, Puchvillers, July 14-16.

Gooderham, 2d. Lt. Rev. Ernest John Robinson Briggs, R. Irish Rifles, Agney, Dec. 13-16.

Goodhart, Comr. Francis Herbert Heaveringham, D.S.O., A.M., R.N., Russian Order of St. George, Legion of Honour, Rev. Charles Alfred Goodhart, Rector of Lambourne, Garelock, Jan. 30-17.

Goodwin, Lt. Bransby William, M.C., South African Infantry, Rev. William Allerton Goodwin, Rector of Queenstown, South Africa, Ypres, Apr. 30-18.

Gordon, Capt. Alexander John Maxwell, London Regt., Rev. Edward George Gordon, Vicar of St. John's, Lambeth, Cambrai, Nov. 27-17.

Gorringe, Mervyn Hugh Egerton, New Zealand E.F., Rev. Peter Rollins Gorringe, Rector of Manston, Etaples, Dec. 19-17.

Gosset, Isaac Charles, N.Z.E.F., Rev. Charles Hilgrove Gosset, Archdeacon of Christchurch, N.Z., Gallipoli, May 2-15.

Gould, 2d. Lt. Henry Charles Hamerton, R.F.A., Rev. Charles Hamerton Gould, Rector of Fawley, Arras, Apr. 15-17.

Gow, Surgeon Charles Humphrey, R.N., Rev. H

Gow, Lt. Roderic Charles Alister, R.N., Rev. James Gow, Head Master of Westminster School, H.M.S. Defence, Jutland, May 31-16.

Grace, Capt. Handley Carleton, Northants Regt., Rev. George Frederick Grace, Vicar of Stanstead Abbots, Courtia, Sep. 2-17.

Graham

Grahame, Francis George, Lincolnshire Regt., Rev. David Francis Alexander Grahame, of St. Anne's, Lincoln, Beckenham, May 21-18.

Gramshaw, Lt. Robert Wilfrid Raleigh, Sussex Regt., Rev. Michael Oginski Gramshaw, of Fittleworth, Bethune, Jan. 27-15.

Grant, Capt. Hubert Anthony, Leicester Regt., Archdeacon Grant, of Aylesford, Loos, Nov. 24-14.

Grasett, Lt. Elliot Blair, 28th Punjabis, Rev. James Elliot Grasett, of Cheltenham, Loos, Sep. 25-15.

Greatorex, Geoffrey William Edward, Australian I.F., Rev. Theophilus Greatorex, Rector of Guildford, Western Australia, Villers Bretonneux, Apr. 24-18.

Green, Lt. Arthur Percival, Norfolk Regt., Rev. William Arthur Green, Rector of Winterton, Albert, July 6-16.

Green, Lt. Denis Noel Tyrrell, Sussex Regt., Rev. Professor Edmund Tyrrell Green, of Lampeter, Gaza, March 26-17.

Greenhow, 2d. Lt. Denys Edward, R.A.F., Rev. Edward Henry Greenhow, Vicar of Chidcock, Abele, March 6-17.

Greenland, Lt. Charles Stirling Walter, Gloucester Regt., Rev. Charles Albert Greenland, of Haywards Heath, Ypres, May 2-15.

Greenup, 2d. Lt. John Bertram, Rifle Brigade, Rev. Albert William Greenup, Si. John's Hall, Highbury, Poelcapple, Oct. 13-17.

Greenwood, Lt.-Col. Leonard Montague, D.S.O., M.C., mentioned in despatches, Durham L.I., Rev. Thomas Greenwood, France, Oct. 7-18.

Gregory, Capt. Reuben Henry, M.C., Sherwood Foresters, Rev. William Henry Gregory, Rector of Kedleston, Wytschaat Ridge, June 8-17.

Grensted, Alfred, Royal Fusiliers, Canon Grensted, of Liverpool, Flers, Sep. 15-16.

Gribble, Olrrement, John, Australian I.F., Rev. Arthur Hazlehurst Gribble, Rector of Coonamble, West Australia, Flers, March 22-17.

Griffin, 2d. Lt. Basil Walker, Lincoln Regt., Rev. Horatio John Griffin, Rector of Broxholme, Passchendale, Dec. 2-17.

Griffin, Randle Newcomb, Canadian E.F., Rev. Horatio John Griffin, Rector of Broxholme, Fresnoy, May 17-15.

Griffith, Lt. Arthur Charles Fleming, R. Welsh Fusiliers, Dean of Llandaff, Villers Outreaux, Oct. 8-18.

Griffith, Capt. Allex, Dorset Regt., Rev. Henry Wager Griffith, Vicar of Thorp Arch, Jabel Hamrin Hills, March 25-17.

Griffith, Paul Howell, Rev. D. Howell Griffith, Rector of Bagillt, Jan. 6-18.

Griffith, 2d. Lt. Thomas Comber, L. North Lancashire Regt., Rev. Charles Edward Osborne Griffith, Vicar of East Barsham, Beresnik, North Russia, July 7-19.

Grigson, Capt. Kenneth Walton, Devon Regt., M.C., Rev. William Shuckforth Grigson, Vicar of Pelynt, July 20-18.

Grigson, 2d. Lt. Lionel Henry Shuckforth, Devon Regt., Canon Grigson, Vicar of Pelynt, Fresnoy, May 9-17.

Grigson, Claude Vivian, R.A.F., Canon Grigson, Vicar of Pelynt, Shorncliffe, Oct. 15-18.

Groser, Noel, Australian I.F., Canon Groser, of Perth, West Australia, Bullecourt, Apr. 2-17.

Grove, Major John Archibald, A.S.C., Rev. William Henry Grove, Rector of Cliffe, Fresnoy, Aug. 10-18.

Grover, Major John, R.M.L.I., Rev. John Grover, of Coventry, Gallipoli, June 24-15.

Grubb, 2d. Lt. Donald James, Royal Inniskilling Fusiliers, Rev. James Grubb, of Belfast, Gallipoli, Aug. 15-15.

Grundy, Lt. George Edward, Warwickshire Regt., Rev. William Grundy, Head Master of Malvern, Gallipoli, July 22-15.

Gubbins, Lt.-Col. Richard Rolls, D.S.O., Mentioned in Despatches, A.Q.M.G., Rev. Richard Shard Gubbins, Rector of Upham, at Sea, Jan. 25-18.

Guest, 2d. Lt. John Eric Cox, Warwickshire Regt., Rev Edward Albert Guest, of Finchley, Vincenza, Sept. 20-18.

Guy, Capt. Christopher Godfrey, R.A.F., Rev. Frederic Godfrey Guy, Vicar of Manea, Wyandaele, Aug. 12-17.

Hackett, 2d. Lt. Henry Robert Theodore, Royal Irish Fusiliers, Rev. Henry Monck Mason Hackett, D.D., Vicar of St. Peter's, Belsize Park, London, Gallipoli, Nov. 2-15.

Hackett, Lt. John, R.N., H.M.S. Nimrod, Rev. John Hackett, Rector of Orlingbury, Garth Castle, Oct. 10-18.

Haden, Frederick Haughton, Rifle Brigade, Rev. Frederick William Haden, Rector of Hule, Monchy, Nov. 4-17.

Hales, Capt. Greville Oxley Brunwin, R.A.F., Canon Brunwin Hales, of Colchester, Vimy Ridge, March 24-17.

Hales, Lt. Henry Tooke Brunwin, Lincoln Regt., Canon Brunwin Hales, of Colchester, Hohenzollern Redoubt, Oct. 13-15.

Hall, Capt. Burton Howard, 98th Infantry, Indian Army, Rev. Samuel Howard Hall, Rector of Sproatley, East Africa, Nov. 4-14.

Hall, Lt. Theodore Newman, Oxford & Bucks L.I., Rev. William Aidan Newman Hall, of St. Philip's, Dorridge, Birmingham, Rouen, Aug. 15-16.

Hall, Rev. William, M.C., Rev. George Rome Hall, Vicar of Birtley.

Halse, 2d. Lt. Lionel William, Gloucesters, Rev. William George Halse, Vicar of Holy Trinity, Bridlington, London, Oct. 17-18.

Hamer, Capt. Arthur Derrick, Manchester Regt., Canon Hamer, Vicar of St. Paul's, Newcastle on Tyne, Mauberg, Nov. 6-18.

Hamilton, Capt. Charles Campbell Henderson, Cameronians, Rev. Charles Greenhill Henderson Hamilton, Rector of St. Mary's, Hamilton, Gallipoli, Aug. 21-15.

Hamilton, Capt. Claud William, R.G.A., Rev. Dr. Hamilton, of. W. Kensington, Ypres, Nov. 6-17.

Hamilton, 2d. Lt. Noel Crawford, Northants Regt., Rev. Dr. Hamilton, of W. Kensington, Trones Wood, July 14-16.

Hamilton, Lt. Herbert Otho, Northumberland Fusiliers, Rev. William Frederick Tucker Hamilton, Vicar of Cromer, Loos, Sept. 26-15.

Hamilton, 2d. Lt. Hubert Arthur, New Zealand E.F., Canon Hamilton, of Canterbury, N.Z., Gallipoli, Aug. 22-15.

Hamilton, Lt. James Campbell Henderson, Black Watch, Rev. Charles Greenhill Henderson Hamilton, Rector of St. Mary's, Hamilton, Loos, Sept. 25-15.

Hamilton, Capt. Harold Gerard Hans, Border Regt., Rev. Charles Hans Hamilton, Vicar of Holybourne, Arras, July 27-17.

Hamilton, Lt. Bernard St. George, M.G.C., Rev. J M, Hamilton, June 28-17.

Hammond, 2d. Lt. Frederick Robert Cyprian, London Regt., Rev. Frederick John Hammond, Vicar of All Hallows, Rochester, Flanders, July 5-15.

Hammonds, Major Denys Huntingford, R.E., D.S.O., M.C., Mentioned in Despatches, Prebendary Hammonds, of Chichester, Hangard, March 30-18.

Hampson, 2d. Lt. Alfred Eric, Cheshire Regt., Rev. Herbert Hampson, Vicar of St. George's, Stalybridge, Thiepval, July 7-16.

Hancock, 2d. Lt. John Maurice, R.A.F., Canon Hancock, Stapleton, Isle of Thanet, March 7-18.

Hanning, 2d. Lt. James Henry Rowland, Lincoln Regt., Rev. Clement Hugh Hanning, Rector of Branston, Loos, Sept. 26-15.

Harbord, Capt. Stephen Gordon, M.C., R.F.A., Rev. Henry Harbord, of Colwood Park, Bolney, Wieltze, Aug. 14-17.

Hare, Wilfrid John, Irish Rifles, Rev. Arthur Henry Maclean Hare, Rector of St. Edmund's, Exeter, Jerusalem, Dec. 23-17.

Harford, Lt. George Lawrence, K. O. Lancashire, Regt., Mentioned in Despatches, Canon Harford, Vicar of Mossly Hill, Ypres, Feb. 17-15.

Harland, Eustace William, R.N.A.S., Rev. William George Harland, Vicar of Lythe, Cranwell, March 18-18.

Harland, Capt. Reginald Wickham, Hampshire Regt., Rev. Albert Augustus Harland, Vicar of Harefield, Ploegsteert, Oct. 30-14.

Harper, 2d. Lt. Charles Croke, Oxford & Bucks L.I., Rev. Edward James Harper, Rector of Broughton, Monchy, May 3-17.

Harper, Maurice H. De, R.N., Rev. Henry Barnett Harper, Vicar of Lesbury, H.M.S. Queen Mary, Jutland, May 31-16.

Harpley, 2d. Lt. Robert Ableson, M.G.C., Rev. Thomas Ableson Harpley, Vicar of St. Lawrence, York, July 5-16.

Harris, Lt. Charles Noel. Napier Rifles, Rev. Dr. Harris, Rector of Colwall, Mesopotamia, Apr. 21-21.

Harris, Capt. Edward, New Zealand E.F., Archdeacon of Akaroa, N.Z., Darnancourt, Sept. 18-16.

Harris, Capt. Ernest Charles, West Riding Regt., Rev. James Harris, Rector of Paglesham, Somme, Oct. 23-16.

Harris, Lt. Ernest Edward, Royal Irish Fusiliers, Rev. Frederick William Harris, of Carlton Road, Putney, Julich, Apr. 21-17.

Harris, Capt. Hubert Alfred, R.A.M.C., Rev. Frederick William Harris of Carlton Road, Putney, Elverdinghe, July 31-17.

Harrison, Major Richard Scorer Molyneux, 51st Sikhs, Rev. Albert Richard Harrison, Vicar of Tettenhall, Gallipoli, Aug. 16-15.

Harrison, 2d. Lt. Leonard John, Lancashire Fusiliers, Rev. Arthur Leonard Harrison, Rector of Yelverton, Ypres, May 24-15.

Harrison, Clarence John, York & Lancaster Regt., Rev., Somme, July 1-16.

Hart, Lt. Charles Crowther, West Riding Regt., Rev. Frederick Hart, Rector of Kimberley, South Africa, East Africa, Nov. 15-17.

Hart, Christodas Frederick, Australian I.F., Rev. Frederick William Hart, Vicar of Coffs Harbour, New South Wales, Gallipoli, May 20-55.

Hart, 2d. Lt. Edgar Oswald, Yorkshire Regt., Rev. Edgar Edward Hart, Vicar of Downholme, Contalmaison, July 10-16.

Hartigan, Lt. Kenneth Leslie Steward, Scinde Horse, Rev. Allen Stewart Hartigan, of St. Leonard's on Sea, Alexandria, Nov. 2-19.

Hartley, Lt. William Ismay Spooner, K. O. Yorkshire L.I., Rev. William Robert Hartley, Rector of Bamburgh, Ovillers, July 1-16.

Harvey, Lt. Frank Lennox, 9th Lancers, Rev. Edward Douglas Lennox Harvey, of Horsham, Messines, Oct. 31-14.

Harvey, 2nd. Lt. Douglas Lennox, 9th Lancers, Rev. Edward Douglas Lennox Harvey ,of Horsham, Messines, Nov. 3-14.

Harvey, Capt. Richard Ernie, Black Watch, Prebendary Harvey, Vicar of Hailsham, Loos, Sept. 25-15.

Harvey, Capt. Rollo Daubigne, Sussex Regt., Prebendary Harvey, Vicar of Hailsham, Somme, Sept. 9-15.

Harvey, 2d. Lt. Ronald Marmaduke Dawney, North Staffordshire Regt., Rev. Frederick Mortimer Harvey, Rector of Bolnhurst, Hill 60, Apr. 20-15.

Harwood,

Hasluck, 2d. Lt. Sydney Vandyke, 14th Sikhs, Rev. Ernest Edward Hasluck, Vicar of Handley, Gallipoli, June 4-15.

Hassall, Robert George, Canadian, E.F., Rev. Thomas Lionel George Hassall, Rector of Rearsby, Bury, Sept. 2-18.

Hastings, Capt. George Herbert, Middlesex Regt., Rev. Samuel Hastings, Vicar of Halton, Armentieres, Feb. 5-15.

Hawkesworth, Lt. Francis Henry Stanley Hawkesworth, Border Regt., Rev. John Hawkesworth, Vicar of Ambleside, Givenchy, Jan. 25-15.

Hawkins, Major Charles Francis, R.F.A., Rev. William Webster Hawkins, Rector of Hinderclay, France, Apr. 25-15.

Hawkins, 2d. Lt. Herbert Edward, London Scottish, Canon Edward Hugh Hawkins, Vicar of Holy Trinity, Stroud, Guemappe, May 13-17.

Haythornthwaite, Lt. Rycharde, Mead, East Kent Regt., Rev. John Parker Haythornthwaite, Vicar of Kings Langley, Ypres, May 24-15.

Hazelton, John Douglas, Canadian E.F., Rev. Edward Hazelton, of Belfast, Arras, June 25-18.

Head, Lt. Basil William, Hertfordshire Regt., Rev. William Head, Rector of Brilley, St. Julien, July 31-17.

Heald, Lt. William Margetson, R.A.M.C., Rev. Charles William Heald, Rector of Chale, Rouen, Sept. 8-18.

Heale, Lt.-Col. Ernest Newton, 121st Pioneers, J.A., Rev. Newton Heale, of St. Margarets on Thames, Le Trepot, June 12-16.

Heale, Capt. George Reginald Charles, Duke of Wellington's Regt., M.C., Mentioned in Despatches, Rev. Newton Heale of St. Margarets on Thames, Fampoux, May 3-17.

Healey, 2d. Lt. Richard Elkanah Hawnam, R. W. Kent, Rev. Randolph Eddowes Healey, Vicar of St. Thomas, Coventry, Somme, July 22-16.

Healy, Lt. George Ernest, R.A.S.C., Canon G. W. Healy, of Cork, Dublin, March 3-19.

Healy, Lt. Guy Rambant, Munster Fusiliers, Archdeacon Healy, of Meath, Lateema Hill, East Africa, March 11-16.

Heard, Capt. Robert James Bannatyne, Lancashire Fusiliers, Prebendary Heard, of Wells, Rector of Caterham, Alexandria, May 4-15.

Hedley, Capt. Gerald Montague, R.E., Rouen, Oct. 4-18.

Hedley, Capt. William Alexander Cosgrave, The Buffs, Rev, Herbert Hedley, Vicar of Nackington, Dickebusch, July 19-18.

Hemphill, 2d. Lt. Richard Patrick, Leinster Regt., Rev. Samuel Hemphill, Archdeacon of Down, Heliopolis, March 24-17.

Hensley, Capt. Wilfrid Henry, Somerset L.I., Rev. Henry Gabriel Hensley, Rector of Gt. Barrington, St. Quentin, March 21-18.

Herdman, Lt. Arthur Widdrington, Shropshire L.I., Rev. Robert Morrison Herdman, Vicar of Holy Trinity, N. Shields, Lille, Oct. 24-14.,

Herford, Lt. Bernard Henry, R.M.L.I., Rev. Percy Michener Herford, Rector of Christ Church, Leith, Gallipoli, May 10-15.

Hervey, 2d. Lt. Thomas Percy Arthur, K.R.R.C., Rev. James Arthur Hervey, Rector of Chipstead, Sept. 15-16.

Hewetson, Capt. Richard John Philip, L.N. Lancashires, Rev. William Hewetson, Vicar of St. Cuthbert's, Bedford, Beauvieux, July 3-18.

Heynes, 2d. Lt. Dudley Hugo, R.F.A., Rev. George Hugo Heynes, of Dunebon, Berkhamstead, Villers, May 16-18.

Hicks, Capt. Edwin Theodore, Lincoln Regt., Bishop of Lincoln, Heilly, May 12-17.

Hicks, 2d. Lt. Harley Lionel Adrian Oswald, Middlesex Regt., Rev. Thomas William Oswald Hicks, Arras, Apr. 12-18.

Hill, Capt. Charles Edward Cecil, Highland L.I., Canon Hill, Rector of Bury, Kut, Apr. 16-16.

Hill, Capt. Charles Edward, Middlesex Regt., Rev. Edward Hill, Vicar of Boxgrove, Hulloch, Sept. 28-15.

Hill, Norman George Tynwald, King's Liverpool Regt., Rev. Oscar Elliott Hill, Rector of Barnoldby le Beck, Guillimont, Aug. 13-16.

Hill, Lt. Col. Collis George Herbert St., Sherwood Foresters, Rev. Warren Woodford St. Hill, Beaucamp, July 8-17.

Hill, Lt. Walter Edward, North Staffordshire Regt., Rev. Charles Rowland Hay dock Hill, Canon of Salisbury, Aisne, Sept. 25-14.

Hilton, 2d. Lt. Henry Denne, Middlesex Regt., Rev. Henry Mosay Hilton, Rector of Orlingbury, Kemmel Hill, Dec. 19-14.

Hinckley, 2d. Lt. Siegfried Thomas, The Buffs, Rev. A. Hinckley, C.M.S., India, July 3-16.

Hind, Capt. Arthur Charles Sinclair, 110th Mahratta L.I., Rev. William Hind, Vicar of St. John's, Hampstead, Mesopotamia, Apr. 14-15.

Hindson, Lt. Leslie Reginald Probyn, R.F.A., Rev. John Hutchinson Hindson, Vicar of Wyrardisbury, Messines, June 10-17.

Hinson, Capt. Heber Basil, N.Z.E.F., Rev. Stanley Hinson, Vicar of Te Ngawai, Christchurch, N.Z., Damascus, March 30-18.

Hipkins, Capt. Frederick Wystans, M.C., Sherwood Foresters, Rev. Frederick Charles Hipkins, of Repton, St. Quentin, Oct. 3-18.

Hipkins, Capt. L. H., Cambridge Regt., Rev. G. H, Hipkins, Oct. 7-18.

Hirst, Lt.-Col. Henry Denne, The Buffs, Rev. T. Hirst, Rector of Bishopsbourne, Dover, May 16-18.

Hobson, Lt. Andrew John Hay, West Yorkshire Regt., Rev. John Phillip Hobson, Vicar of Legbourne, Passchendale, Oct. 9-17.

Hocking, Sub. Lt. William, R.N., Rev. Richard Hocking, Rector of Pillaton, Immingham, April 21-16.

Hodge, Lt. Andrew Brickland, Leinster Regt., Rev. John Macker Hodge, Vicar of St. Luke's, Plymouth, Zillebeke, July 31-17.

Hodge, 2d. Lt. Dorrien Edward Grose, Suffolk Regt., Prebendary Hodge, of St. Paul's, St. Julien, Apr. 27-15.

Hodges, Lt. Eric Colpoys, R. Irish, Rev. Richard James Hodges, Rector of Youghal, Somme, July 15-16.

Hodges, 2d. Lt. Henry Harold, Leinster Regt., Rev. John George Hodges, Rector of Ardnurcher, Co. Meath, Givenchy, July 13-16.

Hodges, Lt. John Cyril, R.G.A., Rev. Edmund James Hodges, Rector of Markshall, Castle Bromwich, Sept., 17-16.

Hodgkinson, Lt. Geoffrey Still, R.F.A., Rev. Frederick Karslake Hodgkinson, Vicar of St. Peter's, Forest Gate, Ypres, July 24-17.

Hodgson, Lt. William Noel, M.C., Devon Regt., Bishop of Edmundsbury and Ipswich, Somme, July 1-16.

Hodgson, 2d. Lt. Cyril Francis, 124, Baluchis, Rev. Francis Douglas Hodgson, Vicar of Worth, Kut, Jan. 11-17.

Hodgson, Geoffrey Mitchel, Canadian E.F., Rev. John Henry Hodgson, of Swanmore, Brise, Oct. 14-15.

Hodgson, Lt. George William Houghton, Border Regt., Rev. William George Courtney Hodgson, Houghton House, Cumberland, Boulogne, Nov. 6-14.

Hodson, Hubert Bernard, Canadian E.F., Rev. Thomas Hodson, Rector of Oddington, Ypres, May 8-15.

Hoffe, Capt. Thomas Mitchell, Cape Corps, Rev. John Hoffe, Rector of Kilbride, Arklow, Doctema, Sept. 23-17.

Hoghton, Brig.-Gen. Frederick A., G.C.S.I., Rev. E. Houghton, Vicar of Woodhouse Eaves, Mesopotamia, May 19-16.

Holbech, 2d. Lt. David, K.R.R.C., Rev. Hugh Holbech, Rector of Bredon, Ypres, Apr. 8-17.

Holden, Lt. Col. Hyla Napier, D.S.O. and Bar, Rev. Oswald Mangin Holden, Rector of Steeple Langford, Aleppo, Oct. 26-18.

Holden, Rev. Oswald Addenbrooke, C.F., Rev. Oswald Mangin Holden, Rector of Steeple Langford, Cambrai, Dec. 1-17.

Hollands, John Rupert Weigall, Canadian E.F., Rev. Charles William Hollands, Rector of Carbonear, Newfoundland, Ypres, Apr. 23-15.

Holies, 2d. Lt. Frederick Tetheslay Noel, E. Lancashire Regt., Rev. Frederick Edward Richard Holies, of Weston-super-Mare, Basra, Sept. 11-16.

Holme, 2d. Lt. George Weston, R.F.A., Rev. George Frederick Holme, Rector of Penshaw, Lonqueval, Dec. 22-16.

Holmes, Rev. E. R. Holmes.

Holt, Eustace Addison, Liverpool Regt., Rev. George Owen Holt, Vicar of Astley, Rouen, Oct. 4-16.

Holt, 2d. Lt. William Leslie, York & Lancaster Regt., Rev. Alfred Holt, Vicar of Oaks, Ypres, Dec. 23-17.

Homan, Capt. Henry Leslie, Middlesex Regt., Canon Homan, of Kingstown, Neuve Chapelle, March 10-15.

Hope, Lt. Reginald Addison, North Staffordshire Regt., Rev. David Hope, Rector of Birnam Wood, Jamaica, Ypres, July 21-17.

Hopkins, Capt. Laurence Hilton, Cambridge Regt., Rev. George Hanslip Hopkins, Rector of Chigwell Row, Arras, Oct. 7-18.

Horn, Lt. Francis Cuthbert, Manchester Regt., Rev. William Horn, Rector of Waltham, Montigney, May 28-18.

Hornabrook, 2d. Lt. Leonard Charles, Australian I.F., Archdeacon of Adelaide, South Australia, Camiers, May 21-18.

Hornby, 2d. Lt. Geoffrey Phipps, Suffolk Regt., Archdeacon of Lancaster, Ypres, May 8-15.

Hornby, 2d. Lt. William, King's Liverpool Regt., Archdeacon of Lancaster, Somme, Oct. 12-16.

Horton, Francis King, Canadian E.F., Rev. Alfred William Horton, Rector of Dewsall, Vimy, March 1-17.

Hoskyns, Major Henry Charles Walter, D.S.O., Leicester Regt., Rev. Charles William Hoskyns, Rector of Holywell Hunts, Loos, Sept. 25-15.

Houghton, Arthur Hamilton, R.N.D., Rev. Arthur Webster Houghton, Vicar of St. Stephen's, Bury, Cambrai, Dec. 19-17.

Houldsworth, 2d. Lt. William Gilbert, Scots Guards, Rev. William Thomas Houldsworth, of Lennox Gardens, Neuilly, Sept. 23-14.

Houston, Lt.-Col. Charles Elrington Duncan Davidson, D.S.O., 58th Rifles, Indian Army, Rev. Bennett Clear Davidson-Houston, Vicar of St. John's, Sandymount, Loos, Sept. 25-15.

How, James Dennison, Canadian E.F., Rev. Henry How, Rector of St. Luke's, Annapolis Royal, Nova Scotia, Merricourt, Sept. 11-17.

Howard, Lt. Henry Charles Mowbray, York & Lancaster Regt., Rev. Henry Frederick Howard, Rector of Brightwalton, Loos, Sept. 25-15.

Howell,

Howis, 2d. Lt. Frank Thackery, Essex Regt., Rev. Charles William Howis, Vicar of Pleshy, Gallipoli, Dec. 8-15.

Hoyle, Lt. Basil William Edmund, Royal Welsh Fusiliers, Rev. Joshua Fielding Hoyle, Rector of Gt. Brickhill, Festubert, Sept. 29-15.

Hudson, Capt. Arthur Hensley, Berks Regt., Rev Thomas William Hudson, Rector of Gt. Shefford, Ypres, July 31-17.

Hudson, Capt. Thomas Heyliger, Berks Regt., Rev. Thomas William Hudson, Rector of Gt. Shefford, Loos, Oct. 13-16.

Hudson, Capt. Austin Patrick, Lancashire Fusiliers, Rev. Richard Plantagenet Hudson, Vicar of St. John's, Bury, Ypres, Aug. 31-17.

Hudson, 2d. Lt. Edward Stanley, Devonshire Regt., Rev. Edward Francis William Hudson, of Saunton, Devon, Doiran, Feb. 13-17.

Hudson, 2d. Lt. Francis Reginald, R.A.F., Rev. Arthur Reginald Hudson, Rector of Huntsham, Biggin Hill, Kent, March 21-18.

Hudson, Lt. Godfrey Durnside, Gloucester Regt., Rev. Arthur Reginald Hudson, Rector of Huntsham, Givenchy, Apr. 12-18.

Hudson, Lt. Alban John Benedict, M.C., Worcester Regt., Rev. Charles Henry Bickerton Hudson, St. Giles, Oxford, Messines, June 7-17.

Hudson, Rev. G. F. Hudson, of Ilfracombe, Messines, June 7-17.

Hudson, Rev. G. F. Hudson, of Ilfracombe,

Hughes, 2d. Lt. Hugh Darrell, R.W. Fusiliers, Canon Hughes, Rector of Llandudno, Basra, Jan. 14-17.

Hughes, Capt. George Augustus, M.C. and Bar, Duke of Wellington's Regt., Rev. William Hughes, Rector of Hawnby, Mormal Forest, Nov. 4-18.

Hughes, Lt. William, M.C., R.A.F., Rev. William Hughes, Rector of Hawnby, Cairo, Nov. 19-18.

Hughes, 2d. Lt. Harold, R.F.A., Rev. William Hughes, Rector of Hawnby, Vimy Ridge, Apr. 23-17.

Hughes, Hugh Alec, Canadian E.F., Rev. Albert Hughes, Vicar of Bucks Mills, Vimy Ridge, May 1-17.

Hughes, Lindlay Filmer, Princess Alexandra's Horse, Rev. John Lewis Hughes, Rector of Woolhampton, Gallipoli, June 1-15.

Hughes, Lionel, New Zealand E.F., Rev. William Henry Hughes, Vicar of St. Hilary, Marazion, Gallipoli, May 30-15.

Hughes, 2d. Lt. Norman Labrey, Devonshire Regt., Rev. Albert Hughes, Vicar of Bucks Mills, Vaga River, North Russia, June 27-19.

Humphreys, Cyril, Australian I.F., Rev. Humphrey Humphreys, Rector of Henllan, Gallipoli, Aug. 28-15.

Humphreys, Henry St. Giles, Rev. Henry James Humphreys, Vicar of Thornley, Lusitania, May 7-15.

Humphreys, Lt. John Theodore Gordon, 40th Pathans, Rev. Henry James Humphreys, Vicar of Thornley, East Africa, July 19-17.

Humphreys, Capt. Noel Forbes, M.C., Tank Corps, Rev. Henry James Humphreys, Vicar of Thornley, Etaples, March 25-18.

Hunt, Capt. Aubrey Noel Carew, Oxford & Bucks L.I., Rev. Robert Walter Carew Hunt, Vicar of Albury, Ecoivres, June 6-16.

Hunt, Walter Michael Carew, Canadian E.F., Rev. Robert Walter Carew Hunt, Vicar of Albury, Birkenhead, Dec. 27-16.

Hunt, Capt. Frederick William, 19th Lancers, I.A., Rev. William Cornish Hunt, Rector of Odell, France, Oct. 31-14.

Huntington, Ernest Henry, Australian E.F., Rev. H. E. Huntington, of Malvern College, Armentieres, Apr. 25-16.

Husband, 2d. Lt. Kenneth, Wilts Regt., Rev. Edgar Bell Husband, Vicar of St. Luke's, Magog, Ontario, St. Quentin, March 28-18.

Hutchison, Lt. Robert Hamilton, Black Watch, Rev. Robert Hutchison, Rector of Wood Eaton, Lens, Oct. 13-15.

Hutton, 2d. Lt. Richard, Leicester Regt., Rev. Joseph Henry Hutton, Rector of West Heslerton, Zillebeke, Nov. 7-14.

Hutton, Rev. Sydney Frederick, Royal Fusiliers, Rev. Frederick Robert Chapman Hutton, Rector of Ashton under Lyne, Somme, Oct 7-16.

Hyde, 2d. Lt. Charles Stuart, West Yorkshire Regt., Rev. Tom Dodsworth Hyde, Vicar of Whitechapel, Serre, July 1-16.

Hyde, Lt. Eustace Emil, Royal Irish Fusiliers, Rev. Tom Dodsworth Hyde, Vicar of Whitechapel, Le Transloy, Oct. 12-16.

Hyde, 2d. Lt. James Charles, Sherwood Foresters, Rev James Bartlet Hyde, Vicar of Matlock Bath, Gonnecourt, July 1-16.

Hyland, Lt. John Edward, R.M.L.I., Rev. John Black Hyland, Rector of Combe Florey, Gallipoli, May 10-15.

Iliff, 2d. Lt. George, R.A.F., Rev. Alfred Iliff, C.M.S., South China, Gitz, Sept. 25-18.

Ingles, Major Alexander Wighton, West Yorkshire Regt., Canon Ingles, of St. Albans, Aisne, Sept. 24-14.

Innes, Lt. Selwyn Long, Royal Lancaster Regt., Rev. Reginald Gipps Long Innes, Ypres, Aug. 4-15.

Ireland, Henry, Canadian E. F. Oct. 29-16.

Irving, Capt. Thomas Henry, Liverpool Regt., Canon Irving, Vicar of Hawkshead, Delville Hill, Aug. 19-16.

Jackson, 2d. Lt. Arthur Gordon, South Lancashire Regt., Rev. Sydney Jackson, of Mitcham, Baghdad, Feb. 25-17.

Jackson, 2d. Lt. Henry Stewart, Yorkshire L.I., Rev. Sydney Jackson, of Mitcham, Somme, July 1-16.

Jackson, Lt.-Col. Cyril Compton, D.S.O., 110th L.I., Indian Army, Rev. Charles Bird Jackson, Rector of Wold Newton, Ctesiphun, Nov. 22-15

Jackson, Capt. Dudley William Gerald, Royal Welsh Fusiliers, Rev. Gerald Henry Jackson, Rector of Hasfield, Etaples, Apr. 13-16.

Jackson, Lt. Edward Phillips, Warwickshire Regt., Rev. William Edward Jackson, Rector of Loughton, Richebourg L'Avoue, May 9-15.

Jackson, Lt. George Olaf Damian Ceadda, Canadian E.F., Rev. Joseph Jackson, Vicar of Lew Bampton, Vimy, Apr. 28-17.

Jackson, Lt. Hugo Anthony Launcelot Ceadda, Canadian E.F., Rev. Joseph Jackson, Vicar of Lew Bampton, Vimy, Apr. 28-17.

Jackson, Lt. Montagu John Vincent, Sherwood Foresters, Canon Jackson, of Bottesford, Notts, Armentieres, Feb. 5-16.

Jacob, Lt. Gwynne, E. Yorkshire Regt., D.C.M., M.M., Rev. David Jacob, Chaplain H.M. Prison, Durham.

Jacques, Lt. Edward William Rigbye, Northants Regt., Rev. William Baldwin Jacques, Rector of Orlingbury, Foureaux, Aug. 16-16.

Jacques, Lt.-Col. Francis Augustus, 14th Sikhs, Canon Jacques, Rector of Brindle, Gallipoli, June 4-15.

James, 2d. Lt. Basil Lister, The Buffs, Rev. Charles Lister James, Vicar of Broadhembury, Dernancourt, Nov. 21-16.

James, 2d. Lt. Kenneth Lister, The Buffs, Rev. Charles Lister James, Vicar of Broadhembury, Arras, May 3-17.

James, Capt. Francis Arthur, Manchester Regt., Rev. Charles Henry James, Vicar of Haigh, Gallipoli, Sept. 18-15.

James, Charles Edward, Middlesex Regt., Rev. Charles Henry James, Vicar of Haigh, Loos, Sept. 28-15.

James, Lt. Frank Clifford, Berkshire Regt., Rev. Hugh Price James, Vicar of Mynyddislwyn, Oppy, May 4-17.

James, Henry, Middlesex Regt., Rev. Charles Henry James, Vicar of Haigh, Guillemont, Aug. 18-16.

James, Lt. George Sydney, Manchester Regt., Rev. Charles Henry James, Vicar of Haigh, Gallipoli, June 4-15

Jameson, Maurice Gurney, Hon. Artillery, C., Rev. Hampden Gurney Jameson, Vicar of St. Peter's, Eastbourne, Ypres, March 6-15.

Jansen, Francis Charles Theodore, Royal Fusiliers, Rev. Francis Charles Theodore Jansen, Vicar of Newton Solney, Pozieres, July 31-16.

Jelf, 2d. Lt. Charles Gordon, The Buffs, Rev. George Edward Jelf, Loos, Oct 13-15.

Jenkins, Lt. David Lewis, Royal Welsh Fusiliers, Rev., Zonnebeke, Sept. 26-17.

Jenkins, Rev. Edward Rupert Menlove,

Jenkins, Capt. Morgan Jones, Canadian E.F., Rev. John Jenkins, Vicar of Llantwit Vairdre.

Jenkins, 2d. Lt. Sidney Emlyn, R. Welsh Fusiliers, Rev. Rhys Jenkins of Tredegar, Somme, April 22-18.

Jennings, 2d. Lt. Goulbourne Hayward, Royal Welsh Fusiliers, Rev. Richard Jennings, Rector of Gyffylliog, France, Aug. 18-16.

Jennings, Lt. Richard William, Worcester Regt., Rev. Arthur Charles Jennings, Rector of Kings Stanley, Somme, July 3-16.

Jepson, Capt. Arthur George Leslie, London Regt., Rev. George Jepson, Rector of Uckfield, Leuze Wood, Sept. 15-16.

Jerram, Midshipman Henry Escombe Ravenhill, R.N., Rev. Arnold Escombe Jerram, of Edgbaston, H.M.S. Hawke, Oct. 15-14.

Jervis, Capt. Arthur Cyril, Liverpool Regt., Rev. John Jervis, Vicar of Snitterfield, East Africa, July 13-18

Jervis, 2d. Lt. John Cedric, Royal Fusiliers, Rev. John Jervis Vicar of Snitterfield, Courcelles, Oct. 26-16.

Jeudwine, Capt. Spencer Henry, Lincolnshire Regt., Archdeacon of Lincoln, Somme, July 1-16.

Job, 2d. Lt. Bernard Craig Keble, West Kent Regt., Rev. Frederick William Job, Vicar of Lower Gornal, Hill 60, Apr. 18-16.

Johns, Lt. Arthur Hugh, R. Sussex Regt., Rev. Roger Owen Johns, Vicar of Billingshurst, Albert, Sept. 1-16.

Johnson, 2d. Lt. Leslie Nethercote, M.C., Sherwood Foresters, Rev. Alfred Henry Samuel Johnson, Rector of Trusley, Lens, July 3-17.

Johnston, 2d. Lt. John Leslie, Oxford & Bucks L.I., Canon Johnston, Sub Dean of Lincoln, Givenchy, May 15-15.

Johnston, Capt. John Lyonel Lukin, Leinster Regt., Rev. Robert Edwin Johnston, Vicar of Harden, Bailleul, June 21-16.

Jones, Lt. Alfred Selwyn Basil, Canadian E.F., Canon Jones, Vicar of Llanfair, Kimmel, Feb. 9-19.

Jones, Archibald Edward, Leicestershire Regt., Rev. Enoch Edward Jones, Rector of Shawell, St. Leger, June 5-17.

Jones, Arthur, K.R.R.C., Canon Jones, of Abergele, Unknown, France, Feb. 19-15.

Jones, 2d. Lt. Arthur Saunders, R.A.F., Rev. William Jones, of Prestatyn, Belgium, Unknown, Sept. 18- .

Jones, Lt. David William Llewelyn, London Regt., Canon David Jones, of Penmaenmawr, July 2-16.

Jones, Capt. Douglas Llewellyn, Lincolnshire Regt., Rev. John David Jones, Vicar of St. Mary's, Lincoln, Langemarck, Aug. 22-17.

Jones, Edgar Wilkinson, York & Lancaster Regt., Canon Jones, of Abergele, Ypres, Apr. 8-17.

Jones, 2d. Lt. Ivor Dryhurst S. Wales Borderers, Rev. William Jones, of Prestatyn, Messines, Apr. 10-18.

Jones, Capt. Edward Thomas, R.A.M.C., Rev. Alfred Jones, Vicar of Kenilworth, East Meon, Feb. 19-19.

Jones, Lt.-Col. Francis George, Inniskilling Fusiliers, Rev. Edward George Jones, of Marlow, Gallipoli, May 5-15.

Jones, 2d. Lt. Frederick Thomas Avery, Herefordshire Regt., Rev. Alexander George Jones, Vicar of Yorkhill, Rouen, Dec. 5-17.

Jones, Capt. Frank M., Royal Fusiliers,

Jones, 2d. Lt. Geoffrey Anthony St. John, Middlesex Regt., Rev. Alfred Henry Jones, Vicar of St. Martin's, Stamford, France, June 14-16

Jones, Gerald Adrian Disney, West Surrey Regt., Rev. J. Jiffares Jones, of Belfast, Achiet le Grant, March 24-17.

Jones, Capt. Gilbert Lloyd Sinnett, Royal Welsh Fusiliers, Rev. James Sinnett Jones, Rector of Caerwys, Mesopotamia, Apr. 9-15.

Jones, 2d. Lt. James Victor Sinnett, Royal Welsh Fusiliers, Rev. James Sinnett Jones, Rector of Caerwys, Mamety Wood, July 10-18.

Jones, Harold Charles, London Regt., Rev. Hugh William Jones, Rector of Llanferres, Givenchy, May 25-15.

Jones, 2d. Lt. Henry St. John Saunders, 20th Punjabis, Rev. David Saunders Jones, Rector of Cantreff, Lindi, Aug. 3-17.

Jones, Herman Hill, Australian I.F., Rev. E. L., Rector of Llansantfraid, June 9-15.

Jones, Lt. Hilary Gresford Evan, Welsh Regt., Canon Evan Jones, of Llanllwchaim, Ypres, Feb. 16-15.

Jones, 2d. Lt. Hywel Herbert Saunders, West Surrey Regt., Rev. John Jones, Rector of Wolves Newton, Peronne, March 4-17.

Jones, Lt. John Harold Ryle, South Lancashire Regt., Rev. John Roger Jones, Vicar of Gt. Sankey, July 4-16.

Jones, Capt. Lawrence Henry, East Surrey Regt., Rev. Gustavus John Jones, Rector of Crayford, Polygon Wood, Oct. 4-17.

Jones, Lt. Morys Wynne, R.E., Rev. John William Wynne Jones, Vicar of Carnarvon, Zendvoorde, Oct. 29-14.

Jordan, 2d. Lt. Percy Thomas, Inniskilling Fusiliers, Prebendary Jordan, of Magherafelt, Gallipoli, Aug. 21-15.

Jose, Lt. Wilfrid Oswald, Australian I.F., Canon Jose, of Adelaide, South Australia, Noreuil, Apr. 3-17.

Jubb, Capt. Cyril Oswald Denman, West Riding Regt., Rev. Henry Denman Jubb, of Bournemouth, Wasmes, Aug. 24-14.

Jukes, Sub.-Lt. Ronald Worthington, R.N.V.R., Rev. Worthington Jukes, Rector of Shobrooke, Gallipoli, June 4-15.

Jump, Stanley, Artists Rifles, Rev. John Edward Jump, Vicar of Laughton en le Morthen, Cambrai, Dec. 30-17.

Kayss, Cadet John Harvey Bainridge, M.M., Canadian, E.F., Rev. John Bainbridge Kayss, Vicar of Wighton, Shorncliffe, March 25-18.

Keable, 2d. Lt. Harold Charles Linford, Royal Berks, Rev. Charles Henry Keable, Vicar of Wrecclesham, Loos, Sept. 25-15.

Keble, 2d. Lt. Eustace Charles, N. Stafford Regt., Rev. Thomas Charles Keble, Vicar of Christ Church, Lichfield, Pontruct, March 21-18.

Keene, Lt. Edgar Ralph Ruck, Royal Welsh Fusiliers, Rev. Edmund Ralph Ruck Keene, Rector of Copford, Richebourg St. Avaast, Jan. 16-16.

Keene, Rev. Benjamin Corrie Ruck, C.F., Rev. Edmund Ralph Ralph Ruck Keene, Rector of Copford, Ypres, Sept. 26-17.

Keene, Oswald Rees, West Riding Regt., Rev. Rees Keene, Rector of Gosforth, Hill 60, May 5-15.

Kelley, Lt. Robert Maitland, Dorset Regt., Rev. Maitland Kelly, Rector of Kelly, Devon, Beaumont Hamel, Jan. 11-17.

Kelly, Rev. Richard Hugh Dickson Kelly, Rector of Millthorpe, New South Wales.

Kemp, 2d. Lt. Norman, Lancashire Fusiliers, Canon Kemp, of Manchester, Ginchy, Sept. 9-16.

Kemp, Capt. Percy Vickerman, Durham L.I., Rev. James Vickerman Kemp, Vicar of Witton Park, Le Touquet, May 31-18.

Kempston, Sergt. James Campbell, Canadian E.F., Rev. William Augustus Kempston, Rector of Bally, Ypres, June 3-16.

Kempthorne, Lt. Harold Simpson, R.F.A., Archdeacon of Waimea, N.Z., France, Aug. 24-17.

Kennaway, Lt. Arthur Lewis, Dorset Yeomanry, Rev. Charles Lewis Kennaway, Vicar of Tarrant Crawford, Gallipoli, Aug. 21-15.

Kennedy, Cadet Herbbert Colles, R.F.A., Very Rev. Herbert Brownlow Kennedy, Dean of Christ Church, Dublin, Brighton, Oct. 15-18.

Kennelly, Lt. Leslie William, R. Sussex Regt., Rev. William James McKeon Kennedy, Canon of Bombay, Oct. 9-15.

Kenny, Eustace Godfrey, Australian I.F., Rev. Robert Kenny, Yorke Peninsula Mission, S Australia, Chateau Foulla, Apr. 20-18.

Kerr, 2d. Lt. George Augustus L'Estrange, Bedford Regt., Rev. George William Kerr, Vicar of St. Mark's, Tollington Park, June 30-18.

Kerridge, Albert Roland, Norfolk Regt., Rev. Albert Alfred Kerridge, Rector of Hawksworth, Hammersmith, March 16-19.

Kerridge, William Alfred, Durham L.I., Rev. Albert Alfred Edward Kerridge, Rector of Hawksworth, Somme, Sept. 10-1S.

Kerrin, Francis, Highland L.I., Rev. Daniel Kerrin, of Aberdeen, Somme, Nov. 18-16.

Kewley, William Christopher, Canadian E.F., Rev. William Kewley, Vicar of Millom, St. Eloi, Apr. 13-16.

Kidson, Lt. Charles Wilfrid, Dublin Fusiliers, Rev. Joseph Charles Eyre Kidson, Vicar of Holy Trinity, Sittingbourne, River Selle, Oct. 17-18.

Killingley, Lt. Hastings Grevatt, Dublin-Fusiliers, Rev. David Francis Killingley, Vicar of Whitechurch, Rathfarnham, Les Boeufs, Oct. 23-16.

King, 2d. Lt. John Stephen, R.A.F., Rev. William Richard Cambridge King, Rector of Swainswick, Cambrai, Oct. 1-18.

King, Rev. Bernard William, K.R.R.C., Rev. William Templeton King, Vicar of Christ Church, Ealing, Mazinghum. Oct. 23-18.

King, Lt. Noel Gilbert Bryan, Wilts Regt., Rev. Gilbert Alfred King, Rector of Easterton, Messines, June 7-17.

King, 2d. Lt. Robert Andrew Ferguson Smyly, Dublin Fusiliers, Very Rev. Richard George Salmon King, Dean of Derry, Boulogne, May 23-15.

King, William Ernest, Australian I. F., Canon King, Rector of Kilcolman, Co. Kerry, Gallipoli, Aug. -15.

King, Gordon Ulick, Cheshire Regt., Canon King, Rector of Kilcolman, Co. Kerry, Mesopotamia, Apr. -16.

Kirby, Ernest Seymour, D.C.M., Rev. Augustus George Kirby, Vicar of South Weald, Edinburgh, Feb. 21-18.

Kirby, Rev, Robert Dorrien, Rev. Augustus George Kirby, Vicar of South Weald, Yule, Illama, New Guinea, Apr. 29-16.

Kitchin, Sub.-Lt. Geoffrey Gordon, R.N., Rev. Walter Kitchin, Vicar of Podington, H.M.S. Queen Mary, May 31-16.

Kite, Capt. Ralph Bertram, M.C., Rev. Joseph Bertram Kite, Vicar of St. Peter's, Ealing, Treport, Dec. 10-16.

Kitson, Major Richard Buffer, Vaughans Rifles LA., Rev. John Buffer Kitson, Rector of Lanreath, Palestine, Nov, 13-17.

Knowles, Claude Leonard, N.Z.E.F., Rev. Walter Frank Knowles, Vicar of Amberley, N.Z., Passchendale, Oct. 12-17.

Lachlan, 2d. Lt. Cecil George, W. Yorkshire Regt., Rev. George Lewis Lachlan, Vicar of Tudely, St. Quentin, Aug. 31-17.

Lafone, Capt. Eric William, M.C., Durham L.I., Archdeacon of Furness, Vicar of Kendal, Asiago, Italy, June 15-18.

Lamb, 2d. Lt. John, R.E., Rev. John Lamb, Rector of Blofield, Ypres, Oct. 17-17.

Lane, Capt. Eric Arthur Milner, Manchester Regt., Rev. Frederick John Lane, Vicar of Humberston, Kut, March 7-16.

Lash, Major Augustus Oliver, R. Irish Rifles, Rev. A. Lash, Rector of Framlingham, Sept. 11-16.

Laurence, 2d. Lt. Dudley Sydney, Rifle Brigade, Rev. Frederick Spencer Lawrence, Vicar of Holy Trinity, Cambridge, Les Boeus, Oct. 23-16.

Lauria, William Denis, K.R.R.C., Rev. John Alexander Lauria, Vicar of Emmanuel, Bolton, Hoog, July 30-15.

Law, 2d. Lt. Charles Lindsey Gwydyr, Suffolk Regt., Rev. Henry Kilburn Law, Rector of Dolton, Hooge Sept. 30-15.

Law, 2d. Lt. Henry Merrik Burrell, R.A.F., Rev. Henry Kilburn Law, Rector of Dolton, Bruay, Aug. 8-16.

Law, Lt. Harry, Mentioned in Despatches, Royal Welsh Fusiliers, Rev. James Henry Adeane Law, Rector of West Felton, London, July, 21-15.

Lawrence, 2d. Lt. Joseph Reginald Mark, E. Surrey Regt., Rev. T. R. Lawrence, Aug. 16-16.

Lawson, Lt. Harry Sackville, R.F.A., Rev. R. Lawson, Feb. 5-18.

Layton, Capt. Roland Churchill, Sherwood Rangers, Rev. William Edward Layton, Vicar of Cuddington, Es Salt, Palestine, Apr. 30-18.

Leadbitter, 2d. Lt. Geoffrey George, Northants Regt., Rev. Dr. William Oram Leadbitter, Rector of West Walton, Palestine, Apr. 19-17.

Learoyd, Lt. Digby Guy, R.E., Rev. Digby Johnson Learoyd, Rector of Debden, Mesopotamia, Dec. 13-17.

Ledger, Lt. Raymond Kerwood, Rifle Brigade, Rev. Charles George Ledger, Vicar of St. Paul's, Hereford, Neuve Chapelle, Apr. 13-15.

Lee Capt. Audley Andrew Dowell, M.C., Leicesters, Rev. Dr. William Benjamin Dowell Lee, of Deytheur, Polygon Wood, Oct. 1-17.

Lee, 2d. Lt. Charles Harold, R.G.A., Rev. George Samuel Lee, Rector of Benniworth, Ypres, Sept. 20-17.

Lee, Capt. Edward, Herts Regt., Rev. Arthur George Lee, Rector of Thrandeston, Thiepval, Oct. 14-16.

Lee, Lt. Richard, Suffolk Regt., Rev. Arthur George Lee, Rector of Thrandeston, Hohenzollern Redoubt, Oct. 13-15.

Lee, Capt. Richard Henry Driffield, Norfolk Regt., Rev. Frederick Lee, Rector of Woodton, June 23-17.

Lee, Lt. Frederick Gurdon Driffield, Norfolk Regt., Rev. Frederick Lee, Rector of Woodton, Farnley Park, March 1-16.

Lee, 2d. Lt. Frederick Henry Norris, Irish Guards, Rev. John Theodore Norris Lee, Vicar of Hatfield Regis, Boulogne, July 4-16.

Leece, 2d. Lt. Frank Ballantyne, West Riding Regt., Canon Leece, Vicar of Rushen, I. of M. Le Transloi, Oct. 12-16.,

Lethbridge, 2d. Lt. Brian Hugh Bridgeman, Bedfordshire Regt., Rev. Bridgeman Herbert Servante Lethbridge, Vicar of St. Luke's, Enfield, Loos, July 19-17.

Lewis, Arthur Edward, Canadian E.F., Dean of Bangor, Oct. -18.

Lewis, Arthur Trevor, Gloucester Regt., Canon Lewis, of Ruabon, Birmingham, Apr. 5-18.

Lewis, 2d. Lt. Douglas David Raymond, Durham L.I., Rev. Thomas Phillips Lewis, Vicar of Silian, Arras, Apr. 22-17.

Lewis, 2d. Lt. Edwin Richard Hampton, Worcester Regt., Rev. Edwin Lewis, Rector of Hampton Lovett, Monchy, Apr. 25-17.

Lewis, 2d. Lt. John Walter, Devonshire Regt., Rev. Walter Allen Lewis, Rector of Goodleigh, Somme, July 15-16.

Lewis, Capt Arthur Milton, 53rd Sikhs, Rev. Walter Allen Lewis, Rector of Goodleigh, Mesopotamia, Aug. 8-19.

Lewis, Rev. Ivor Morgan, Chaplain R.N., Rev. David Lewis, Rector of Llanbedr, H.M.S. Goliath, May 13-15.

Lewis, John Gordon, London Regt., Rev. David Lewis, Rector of Llanbedr, Messines, June 7-17.

Lewis, John Theodore Mitchinson, M.G.C., Rev. William John Lewis, Rector of Eydon, Ypres, Aug. 1-17.

Lewis, William Ewart Martin, R.H.A., Rev. William John Lewis, Rector of Eydon, St. Quentin, March 31-18.

Ley, John William, London Regt., Artist Rifles, Rev. Gerald Lewis Henry Ley, Rector of Chagford, Bapaume, Dec. 30-17.

Lias, Lt. Ronald John Mortlock, Sussex Regt., Rev. John James Lias, Chancellor of Llandaff, Ypres, Feb. 23-16.

Lillie, Major Frederick Sutherland, Royal Irish Regt., Rev. John Edward Sutherland Lillie, Rector of Wakes Colne, St. Eloi, March 15-15.

Line, 2d. Lt. Eric Alfred Thiselton, A.S.C., Archdeacon of Waterford, Salonika, Dec. 16-16.

Line, Lt. John Young Alexander, N. Stafford Regt., Rev. John Russell Line, Vicar of Deane, Neuve Chapelle, March 13-16.

Liptrott, Lt. Eric Carr, 6th Jats, Rev. Boulton Brander Liptrott, Vicar of St. James', Teignmouth, Boulogne, Nov. 26-14.

Littlehales, Richard, Grenadier Guards, Rev. Walter Gouth Littlehales, Rector of Balvan, Netley, June 13-15.

Littlewood, Arthur Francis Bewicke, Hon. Artill. C., Rev. Elijah Harrison Littlewood, Vicar of Biggleswade, Etaples, July 7-15.

Livingstone, Capt. Frank Darley, R.A.S.C., Canon Livingstone, of Bristol, Achincourt, March 22-18.

Lloyd, Gilbert Lewis, A.S.C., Rev. William Robert Lloyd, Vicar of Llanstephen, France, Nov. 30-17.

Lloyd, H. George Otway, Canadian E.F., Rev. William Battersby Lloyd, Rector of Rathmullen, Vimy, Feb. 19-17.

Lloyd, Capt. Thomas Glyn, Welsh Fusiliers, Archdeacon of St. Asaph, Vicar of Rhyl, Albert, May 10-18.

Lomas, Lt. George Guest, Manchester Regt., Rev. George Lomas, of Cannock, Staffs, March 22-18.

Longmore, Robert Wilfrid, Canadian E.F., Rev. Francis Longmore, Rector of Carman, Manitoba, Cambria, Sept. 29-18.

Longmore, Alfred Edwin, Canadian E.F., Rev. Francis Longmore, Rector of Carman, Manitoba, Winnipeg, March 29-16.

Longsdale, Lt. Arthur Carr Glynn, K.R.R.C., Rev. John Henry Lonsdale, Rector of Fontmell Magna, Neuve Chapelle, March 10-15.

Loring, Major Charles Buxton, 37th Lancers, I.A., Rev. Edward Henry Loring, Vicar of Gillingham, Givenchy, Dec. 22-14.

Loring, Lt.-Col. Walter Latham, Warwickshire Regt., Rev. Edward Henry Loring, Vicar of Gillingham, Becelacre, Oct. 24-14.

Loring, Capt. William, D.C.M., Scottish Horse, Rev. Edward Henry Loring, Vicar of Gillingham, Gallipoli, Oct. 24-15.

Loveband, Col. Arthur, C.M.G., Dublin Fusiliers, Rev. Anthony William Loveband, of Totnes, Ypres, May 24-15.

Loveband, Capt. Arthur Reginald, West Yorkshire Regt., Rev. Thomas Loveband, Vicar of Burrington, Armentieres, Dec. 6-14.

Loveband, Lionel, Australian I.F., Rev. Matthew Thomas Loveband, Vicar of Burrington, Palestine.

Low, 2d. Lt. Eustace Bertram, R.A.F., Rev. Arthur Edward Low, Vicar of St. John's, Folkestone, March 24-17,

Lowe, Lt. Henry Stanley, Worcester Regt., Rev. E. J. Lowe, Vicar of Stallingborough, Paris, Oct. 21-14.

Loxley, Major Vere Duncombe, R.M.L.I., Rev. Arthur Smart Loxley, Vicar of Fairford, Somme, Nov. 13-16.

Loxley, Capt. Arthur Noel, R.N , Rev. Arthur Smart Loxley, Vicar of Fairford, H.M.S. Formidable, Jan. 1-15.

Loxley, Capt. Reginald Victor Byron, R.A.F., Rev. Arthur Smart Loxley, Vicar of Fairford, Paris, Oct. 18-18.

Luard, Col. Frank William, R.M.L.I., Rev Bixby Garnham Luard, Rector of Birch, Gallipoli, July 12-15.

Lunn, Lt. Herbert Charles, Royal Scots, Rev. Herbert Lunn, Vicar of Chillignham, Arras, March, 21-17.

Lutener, 2d. Lt. Richard Arthur Maurice, Shropshire L.I., Rev. C. Lutener, Vicar of Clun. Apr, 20-16.

Lyon, Lt. Lawrence Gordon, Canadian E.F., Rev. Paul Kemp Lyon, Rector of Lower Sapey, Hindenberg Line, Sept. 11-18.

Lys, 2d. Lt. Francis George Brian, Northants Regt., Rev. Alleyne Fitzherbert Lys, Chaplain in India, Somme, July 14-16.

Lysons, Major Nigel Lucius Samuel, Lancaster Regt., Canon Lysons, of Gloucester, Vicar of Rowsley, France, Oct. 21-14.

Lythgoe, 2d. Lt. Jeffery Wentworth, Royal Warwickshire Regt., Rev. George Edward Lythgoe, Vicar of St. Paul's, Tipton, Somme, July 22-16.

McCarthy, 2d. Lt. William Ranald Ware, Border Regt., Rev. William McCarthy, Vicar of Christchurch, Luton, Gaza, Nov. 2-17.

McClenaghan, 2d. Lt. Arthur Bryant Phelps, Wilts Regt., Rev. George Richard McClenaghan, of Ipswich, Hooge, June 16-15.

McClenaghan, Capt. George Mayo, R. West Kent Regt., Rev. George Richard McClenaghan, of Ipswich, Nov. 8-18.

Maccoll, 2d. Lt. Malcolm Graeme, Australian I.F., Rev. Malcolm Maccoll, Rector of St. Columba, Yoker, Queensland, Bullecourt, May 3-17.

Machell, Lt.-Col. Percy Wilfrid, C.M.G., D.S.O., Border Regt., Canon Machell, of Hull, July 1-16.

Mack, 2d. Lt. Edgar Geoffrey, Wilts Regt., Rev. Edgar Shepheard Paston Mack, of Swanmore, Hants, Hulluch, Sept. 27-15.

Mackain, Capt. James Fergus, 34th Sikhs, Rev. William James Mackain, Vicar of Poslingford, Festubert, Nov. 23-14.

Mackay, Lt. Arnold Langley, Scots Fusiliers, Rev. Angus Mackav, Rector of Holy Trinity, Edinburgh, Le Touquet, Oct. 31-16.

Mackie, Walter Lock Canadian E.F., Rev. Edmund St. Gascoigne Mackie, of Hordle, Hants, Somme, Oct 2-16.

Macklin, 2d. Lt. David, Bedford Regt., Rev. Herbert Walter Macklin, Rector of Houghton, Conquest, March 27-18.

MacLaurin, Cadet John Henry, R.A.F., Canon MacLaurin, of Killaloe, Wittering, Sept. 29-18.

Maciaverty, Capt. Colin Johnstone, Shropshire L.I., Rev. Alexander Maclaverty, Vicar of Llangattock, Leuze, Sept. 18-16.

Maclean, Lt. Arthur Kirkpatrick, Argyll & Sutherland Highlanders, Rev. George Gavin Maclean, Vicar of Wadhurst, Le Cateau, Aug. 26-14.

Maclean, Capt. A., Argyll & Sutherland Highlanders, Mons.

McConnell, Lt. Horace Lincoln Cyril, R.E., Rev. Charles James McConnell, Rector of Pylle, Damascus, Nov. 24-17.

McKenzie, Lt. Kenneth Nowell, East Yorkshire Regt., Rev. Donald James MacKenzie, Canon of Lahore, Gallipoli, June 4-15.

Maclear, Lt. Basil George Hope, M.C., Grenadier Guards, King's School, Canterbury, July 25-15.

Maclear, Lt. Geoffrey d'Olier, Garkwell Rifles, M.C., King's School, Canterbury, Jan. 29-19.

Macleod, Lt. Ian Brace, Black Watch, Rev. Roderick Charles Macleod, Vicar of Milford, Vielle Chapelle, Apr. 17-15.

Macmichael, Rev. William Fisher Macmichael, Vicar of Lee.

Macnicol, 2d. Lt. Horace Bonar, Royal Scots, Rev. H. Macnicol, of Grange Church, Edinburgh, July 30-15.

Macully, Arnold Alexander, Australian, I.F., Rev. Alexander Macully, Vicar of Brighton, South Australia, Premont, Oct. 23-18.

Madden, Lt. Thomas Hilton, Liverpool Regt., Archdeacon Madden, of Liverpool, Givenchy, March 10-15.

Madden, Capt. William Henry, Royal Irish Fusiliers, Dean of Cork, St. Quentin, March 24-18.

Maddox, 2d. Lt. John Mortimer, Lancashire Fusiliers, Rev, John Mortimer Maddox, Vicar of St. Mark's, Bury, Deville Wood, Aug. 12-16

Maddrell, Lt. John Denys Hugh, D.C.L.I., Canon Maddrell, Vicar of Gulval, Le Touquet, Dec. 13-16.

Mahood, Hubert John, Canadian E.F., Rev. John Samuel Mahood, Vicar of Kokanee, British Columbia, Arleux, Apr. 28-17.

Mainprice, Bernard Paul, Assistant Paymaster R.N., Rev. William Mainprice Vicar of Wisborough, H.M.S. Bulwark, Nov. 25-14.

Mainprice, Ernest William Loxley, Fleet Paymaster R.N., Rev. William Mainprice, Vicar of Wisborough, H.M.S. Invincible, Jutland, May 31-16.

Mangin, Lt.-Col. Frederick Meredith, R.A.M.C., King's School, Canterbury, Meerut, Dec. 31-18.

Manley, 2d. Lt. Charles Percival Henry, M.C., R. West Kent Regt., Rev. Charles Augustus Manley, Vicar of St. Dunstan's, Canterbury, Wimereux, Oct. 4-18.

Manley, Capt. David Henry George, Royal Welsh Fusiliers, Rev. Henry Jones Manley, Rector of Llanbedrog, Palestine, Nov. 6-17.

Marchant, Lt.-Col. Louis St Gratien Le, D.S.O., East Lancashire Regt., Rev. Robert Le Marchant, Rector of Little Rissington, Jouane, Sept. 9-14.

Margetts, John Theodore Cameron, West Yorkshire Regt., Rev. William John Margetts, Vicar of Beckford, Ypres, Dec. 10-15.

Marjoribanks, Capt. A., 52nd Sikhs, Rev. Dr. Marjoribanks, of Stenton, Dalta Khaye, Sept. 9-14.

Marriott, Lt. Richard Henry, M.C., Shropshire L.I., Canon Marriott, Rector of Redhill, Somme, Sept. 18-16.

Marriott, 2d. Lt. John Douglas, Cameronians, Rev. Frank Ransome Marriott, Vicar of Wootton, Sept. 26-17.

Marris, Lt. Horace Frost, M.C., R.E., Rev. Charles Colquhourn Marris, Vicar of Habrough, Cambrai, Dec. 12-17.

Marrs, 2d. Lt. Frederick Mallinson, Worcester Regt., Rev. F. Marrs, Mar. 4-17.

Marsden, Lt. Wallace Austin Jonathon, R.A.F., Rev. Jonathan Marsden, Vicar of Llanllwch, Somme, Sept., 24-16.

Marshall, Capt. John Edward, Duke of Cornwall's L.I., Canon Marshall, of Ely, Kemmell, March 30-15.

Marshall, Capt. Evelyn Saffrey, R. Warwickshire Regt., Canon Marshall, of Ely, Orah, Mesoptamia, Apr. 6-16.

Marshall, 2d. Lt. Roger Charles, R.A.F., Rev. Frederick Charles Marshall, Rector of Doddington, Jan. 7-18.

Marson, Lt. John Charles, Welsh Regt., Rev. Claud Latimer Marson, Vicar of Hambridge, Gallipoli, Aug. 7-15.

Martin, Lt.-Col. Aylmer Richard Sanction, Lancashire Regt., Rev. H. Martin, Vicar of Thatcham, Fregenberg, May 8-15.

Martin, Lt. Basil Cuthbert Danvers, Worcester Regt., Rev. Henry Basil Martin, Rector of Pudleston, Gallipoli, June 4-15.

Martin, Francis Aubrey Dunstan, N.Z.E.F., Rev. Francis White Martin, Vicar of Waipukurau, N.Z., Gallipoli, Apr. 30-15.

Martin Albert, Percival, York & Lancaster Regt., Rev. William Alfred Martin, Vicar of Emmanuel, Sheffield, Armentieres, Sept. 25-15.

Martin, 2d. Lt. Francis Henry, R.E, Rev. John Martin, Vicar of Granborough, Gouzeaucourt, Nov. 24-17.

Martin, Capt. John Kingsley, Durham L.I., Canon Martin, of Durham, Rector of Kelloe, Hooge, Aug. 1-15.

Martin, 2d. Lt. Lawrence Henry, Royal Irish Fusiliers, Rev. Richard D'Olier Martin, of Killeshandra, Co. Cavan, Cambrai, Nov. 23-17.

Martin, 2d. Lt. Sidney Grant, R.F.A., Rev. Grantley Clarke Martin, Rector of Stoke, Somme, Apr. 18-17.

Mason, Lt. Gerald Francis, Hampshire Regt., Rev. Charles Arthur Mason, Vicar of Kingsley, Wareham, Sept. 1-17.

Masters, Capt. Bruce Swinton Smith, M.C., Essex Regt., Rev. John Ernest Smith Masters, Vicar of South Banbury, Le Bizet, July 1-16.

Masters, Lt, George Arthur Smith, Bedfordshire Regt., Rev. John Ernest Smith Masters, Vicar of South Banbury, Dramoutre, Aug. 19-15.

Mather, Capt. John Wilfrid, North Lancashire Regt., Rev. Frank Albert Mather, Vicar of Yatton, Gallipoli, Aug. 10/15.

Matheson, 2d. Lt. Claud Bruce, Rifle Brigade, Rev. John Matheson, of Straithnairn, Warneton, Sept. 24-17.

Maughan, 2d. Lt. Alfred William, R.G.A., Rev. John Archibald Colingwood Maughan, Vicar of Prudhoe on Tyne, Messines, June 24-17.

May, 2d. Lt. Paul Archer, Devons, Rev. Frederick Granville May, Rector of Cardynham, Givenchy, Apr. 14-17.

May, 2d. Lt. Thomas Radcliffe Agnew, R.A.F., Rev. Frederick Granville May, Rector of Cardynham, Sangatte, Aug. 9-18.

Mayo, Lt. William Charles, Sherwood Foresters, Rev. Dr. James Mayo, Trinity College, Cambridge, Gallipoli, Aug. 9-15.

Mayo, Capt. Alexander John, R.A.F., Rev. Dr. James Mayo, Trinity College, Cambridge, Brie, Aug. 9-18.

Mead, Capt. Clarence Gawler, M.C., Canadian E.F., Rev. Richard Gawler Mead, Rector of Balcombe, Jan. 18-18.

Meade, 2d. Lt. Wakefield Walde, Worcester Regt., Rev. Wakefield Suft Meade, Rector of Loddington, Hooge, June 20-15.

Mears, 2d. Lt. Edward de Quincey, Essex Regt., Rev. Edward Mears, Rector of Little Bardfield, Trones Wood, July 14-16.

Medd, Alfred Wooldridge, West Surrey Regt., Canon Medd, of Gloucester, Ouderdom, Sept. 5-18.

Melliss, Lt. Andrew Douglas John, Oxford & Bucks L.I., Rev. Andrew Melliss, Vicar of Gawcott, Ypres, Oct. 17-15.

Mellor, Lt. Frederick Courtney, Canadian E.F., Rev. Thomas Crewe Mellor, Rector of St. Luke's, Annapolis, Royal, Nova Scotia, Beaumont Hamel, July 1-16.

Meredith, Maurice Neville, Mysore Lancers, M.C., Rev. William Henry Fitzgerald Meredith, Vicar of Neen Savage, Aleppo, Oct. 26-18.

Merewether, Capt. Christopher Ken, Wilts Regt., Canon Merewether, of St. Thomas', Salisbury, Port Said, Dec. 20-17.

Merriman, 2d. Lt. Charles Henry, Wilts. Regt., Canon Merriman, Rector of Hulme, Arras, Apr. 9-17.

Mertens, Hugh G, London Regt., Rev. Rowland Deane Mertens, Vicar of Arlington, Bray, Aug. 10-18.

Methuen, Lt. John Arthur Paul, Canadian E.F., Rev. Stephen Methuen, Rector of Vange, Doullens, July 20-18.

Middlemis, Lt. Thomas Elmslie, R.F'.A., Rev. John Thomas Middlemiss, of West Didsbury, Ypres, Oct. 17-17.

Mildmay, 2d. Lt. Bouverie Walter St. John, R.F.C., Rev. Arundell St. John Mildmay, Vicar of Wolverton, Doullens, Apr. 16-18.

Miles, Capt. Harry Godfrey Massey, M.C., R.A.M.C., Rev. Joseph Henry Miles, Rector of Pangbourne, Rouen, Apr. 26-18.

Miles, 2d. Lt. Henry Robert, Connaught Rangers, Rev. Philip Edvard Miles, Rector of Odstock, Loos, July 18-16.

Millard, Major Harold, Northants Regt., Rev. Frederick Millard, Chaplain at Havre, Lens, Apr. 12-17.

Millard, Cadet Harold, R.A.F., Rev. Frederick Luke Holland Millard, Vicar of St. Aldan's, Carlisle, Stockbridge, Oct. 17-18.

Milller, Edward Minty, London Regt., Archdeacon of Colombo, Beaumont Hamel, Nov. 13-16.

Milliug, Charles Cyril, New Zealand E.F., Rev. Matthew John Tyne Milling, Vicar of Ashton Keynes, Gallipoli, Aug. 28-15.

Millington, Herbert Hugh, London Irish Rifles, Rev. William Millington, Rector of Cottingham, Ypres, May 14-15.

Mills, Major Gerald Dermond, Sherwood Foresters, Rev. William Mills, Rector of Bennington, Doullens, May 19-17.

Mills, George Merriman Godwin, Rev. William Hathorn Mills, San Bernardino, California.

Mitchell, 2d. Lt. Eric Arthur, South Lancashire Regt., Rev. William Mann Mitchell, Vicar of Elson, Neuve Chapelle, Oct. 27-14.

Mocatta, 2d. Lt. Robert Menzies, R. Welsh Fusiliers, Rev. Henry Elias Mocatta, of Prestatyn, Suvla Bay, Aug. 10-15.

Mogg, Lt.-Com. Henry Raymond Clifton, R.N., Rev. W. Clifton Mogg, of Newbridge on Wye, Shotley, Nov. 2-15.

Mogg, Capt. Cyril Knox Barrow, Canadian E.F., Canon Mogg, Vicar of Bishop's Cannings, Passchendale, Nov. 11-17.

Mogg, Aubrey Barrow, Canadian E.F., Canon Mogg, Vicar of Bishop's Cannings, St. Eloi, Aug. 19-16.

Mogridge, 2d. Lt. Basil Lullelove West, Leicester Regt., Rev. Henry Twells Mogridge, Vicar of Sealford, Hohenzollern Redoubt, Oct. 13-15.

Molloy, Lt. Michael Vallancey, Sherwood Foresters, Rev. Ebon Molloy, Vicar of Shenstone, Hooge, Aug. 9-15.

Moneypenny, John Howard, Canadian E.F., Rev. Phillips Howard Monypenny, Vicar of Hadlow, France, Oct. 16- .

Montgomery, Lt. Neville, Canadian E.F., Rev. Ferguson John Montgomery, Rector of Halse, Lens, Aug. 21-17.

Montgomery, Lt.-Col. Hugh Ferguson, C.M.G., D.S.O., Legion of Honour, R.M.L.I., Rev. Ferguson John Montgomery, Rector of Halse, Dublin, Dec. 10-20.

Moody, Capt. Ambrose, Dorset Regt., Rev. William Herbert Moody, Rector of Bentley, Gallipoli, Aug. 21-15.

Moody, 2d Lt. Charles Angelo, R.F.C., Rev. Henry Moody, Vicar of Welshampton, Aug. 21-17.

Moor, Lt. Christopher, Hampshire Regt., Rev. Charles Moor, Vicar of Barton on Humber, Canon of Lincoln, Gallopili, Aug. 6-15.

Moore, 2d. Lt. Walter Ettrick, Lancashire Fusiliers, Rev. George Moore, Vicar of Packington, Le Cateau, Nov. 8-18.

Moore, Cyril George Ettrick, Canadian E.F., Rev. George Moore, Vicar of Packington, Ypres, June 14-16.

Moore, Lt. Dacre William, Machine Gun Corps, Bishop of Kilmore, Thiepval Wood, June 11-16.

Moore, Lt.-Col. Henry Glanville Allen, East Yorkshire Regt., Rev. Henry Dawson Moore, Vicar of Hornby, Gallipoli, Aug. 7-15.

Moore, Lt. John Aubrey, South Staffordshire Regt., Rev. Herbert Augustine Moore, Rector of Bewdley, Gallipoli, Aug. 19-16.

Morgan, Rev. Walter Giles Morgan, Vicar of St. Stephen's, Norwich.

Morgan, Capt. John Towlson, R.A.F., Rev. Ernest Arundell Morgan, Vicar of St. Andrew's, Willesden, Oct. 29-18.

Morgan, Lt.-Col. John William Moore, D.S.O., Mentioned in Despatches, Royal Irish Fusiliers, Rev. Canon W. Moore Morgan, of Armagh, March 30-17.

Morgan, Lt. Arthur Conway Osborne, R.F.A., Rev. Henry Arthur Morgan, Master of Jesus College, Cambridge, Hohenzollern Redoubt, Oct. 13-15.

Morgan, Eric Fennell Trevor, Manchester Regt., Rev. Henry Morgan, Rector of Holy Trinity, Newport, Mon., Woolwich, Aug. 23-14.

Moriarty, 2d Lt James, Henry R.G.A., Rev.

Morrice, Capt. William Walter, Wilts Regt., Rev. John David Morrice, Rector of St. Edmund's, Salisbury, Ypres, Dec. 30-17.

Morris, Lt. Herbert, Gloyne Forster, South Wales Borderers, Rev. Herbert Forster Morris, Rector of South Hill, Le Treport, Oct. 10-15.

Morris, James Outram, Artist Rifles, Rev. William Morris, Vicar of Sydenham, Oct. -17.

Morris, 2d. Lt. Herbert Gloyne Forster, S. Wales Borderers, Rev. Herbert Forster Morris, Rector of South Hill, Oct. 10-15.

Mortimer, Capt. Gerald Henry Walter, 10th Jats, Canon Mortimer of Lichfield, Festubert, Nov. 23-14.

Moss, Lt. Cyril Gower Vincent Runnels, R.A.F., Rev. Arthur Runnels Moss, Vicar of St. John's, Birmingham, Poelcapelle, Dec. 5-17.

Moss, 2d. Lt. Eric Cross Arnold Runnels, R.F.A., Rev. Arthur Runnels Moss, Vicar of St. John's, Birmingham, Mayence, July 9-18.

Mothe, Lt. Claude Douglas Fenelon do la, R.N.R., Rev. C. H. de la Mothe, Beaumont Hamel, May 7-16.

Mouritz, 2d. Lt. Cecil John Hastings, Leinster Regt., Rev. Francis Stafford Mouritz, Rector of Mayne, Westmeath, Flanders, Dec. 5-16.

Mowbray, Lt. Kenneth John Wharton, Suffolk Regt., Rev. John Robert Wharton Mowbray, Rector of Toppesfleld, Apr. 9-17.

Moxley, 2d. Lt. John Hewitt Sutton, Bedfordshire Regt., Rev. J. H. Sutton Moxley, C.M.F., Ypres, March 13-15.

Moxon, 2d. Lt. Hugh Cecil, Bedfordshire Regt., Rev. Ernest Arthur Moxon, Vicar of All Saints, Newmarket, Philossphe, July 19-17.

Mumford, Henry Walter, London Regt., Rev. Henry Levy Mumford, of Baildon, Arras, Apr. 29-17

Munby, Lt. Ernest John, M.E., Rev. George Woodhouse Munby, Rector of Turvey, Bethune, Jan. 31-15.

Munn, Sergt. Alban Shepherd, Australian I.F., Rev. Joseph Shepherd Munn, Vicar of Orleton, Gallipoli, May 2-15.

Muriel, Barnard John, Norfolk Regt., Rev. Harvey Muriel, Rector of Edingthorpe, Aegean Sea, Aug. 13-15.

Muriel, Capt. Sidney Herbert Foster, Border Regt., Rev. William Carter Muriel, Vicar of Fulham, Gallipoli, Apr. 30-15.

Murphy, Lt. Christopher Fowler, Oxford & Bucks L.I., Canon R. W. Murphy, of Tuam, Ypres, Oct. 20-14.

Murphy, 2d. Lt. James Neville Herbert, Dublin Fusiliers, Rev. W. A. E. Murphy, of Desertmartin, Ypres, May 10-15.

Murray, 2d. Lt. Edward Douglas, Black Watch, Rev. R. P. Murray, Rector of Waddesdon, Somme, July 20-16.

Murray, Lt. Leonard, Lancashire Yeomanry, Rev. Douglas Stuart Murray, Rector of Blithfield, Harlaxton, March 13-17.

Murray, Lt. Maurice Austin, Essex Regt., Rev. Alexander William Oliphant Murray, Rector of Chignal, Loos, Sept. 27-15.

Mylne, Capt. Edward Grahame, Irish Guards, Bishop Mylne, Rouen, May, 13-15.

Mylne, Lt. Ewan Lewis, M.C. Irish Guards, Bishop Mlyne, Les Boeufs, Sept. 15-16.

Nash, Capt. Charles Frederick Wylrow, M.C., Rev. Charles Barnett Nash, Vicar of Watton, Albert, March 27-18.

Nash, Capt. Francis Henry, M.C., North Staffordshire Regt., Rev. Francis Lochie Nash, Vicar of Lane End, Kemmel, July 17-17.

Nash, Lt. Thomas Stuart, R.A.F., Rev. Cecil William Nash, of Kincardine O'Neil, Vignacourt, Aug. 9-18.

Nason, 2d. Lt. Richard Philip, South Notts Hussars, Rev. Richard Muriel Nason, Rector of Saintbury, Kemal, Apr. 16-18.

Nesbit, Cuthbert William, Lincolnshire Regt., Rev. John William Nesbit, Rector of Loudborough, Doullens, Apr. 11-18.

Nevinson, 2d. Lt. Humphrey Kaye Bonney, Manchester Regt., Rev. Thomas Kaye Bonney, Nevison, Rector of Medbourne, Gallipoli, June 5-15.

Newman, Arthur Maurice Tweed, London Regt., Rev. Arthur Edwin Tweed Newman, Vicar of St. Andrews, Whittlesey, May 9-15.

Newton, Lt. Murray Edeil, R.A.F., Rev. George Herbert Newton, Vicar of Wisborough, Messines, June 18-17.

Nicholl, Lt. Christopher Benoni, Canadian E.F., Rev. Edward Powell Nicholl, Vicar of Ascot, Bailleul, July 30-15.

Nicholls, Capt. Douglas William Arthur, M.C., Suffolk Regt., Rev. Francis Hamilton Nicholls, Vicar of St. Maty's, Ipswich, Arras, Apr. 10-17.

Nicolls, Capt. Richard Jefferys, Sherwood Foresters, Rev. Edward Richard Jefferys Nicolls, Rector of Trowell, Le Sars, Oct. 1-16.

Nisbet, Capt. Frank Scobell, Manchester Regt., Canon Nisbet, Rector of Ickham, Le Cateau, Aug. 26-14.

Nixon, Capt. William Eric, K.O. Scottish Borderers, Rev. William Henry Nixon, Vicar of Winster, Masny, May 7-17.

Noble, Mark Athel Chadwick Edgar, Army Ordnance Corps, Rev. Mark Athel Noble, Rector of East Acklam, Alexandria, Apr. 30-17.

Noon, Capt. Alfred Lewis, Devons, Rev. Francis Harold, Vicar of West Hanney, Haplincourt, Apr. 2-18.

Norman, Lt. Alfred George Bathurst, Rev. Harry Bathurst Norman, of Brighton.

Norris, Capt. Gilbert Hume, K.R.R.C., Rev. William Burrell Norris, Rector of Warblington, Italy, March 9-18.

Northcote, 2d. Lt. Hugh Farrar, I.A., R.O., Prebendary Northcote, Mesopotamia, Apr. 28-16.

Northey, Lt. Alfred, Worcester Regt., Rev. Alfred Edward Northey, Vicar of Rickmansworth, Richebourg St. Avaast, Oct. 12-14.

Northey, Major William, D.S.O., Durham L.I., Rev. Edward William Northey, of Woodcote House, Epsom, Ennetiere, Oct. 22-14.

Norton, Cecil Herbert, Canadian E.F., Rev. Philip Norton, Rector of Brindon Parva, Ypres, Apr. 24-15.

Noyes, 2d. Lt. Claude Robert Barton, Lancashire Fusiliers, Rev. Henry Edward Noyes, Vicar of St. Maty's, Kilburn, Bombay, Sept. 5-16.

Noyes, Capt. Francis Golding, R.A.M.C., Rev, Henry Edward Noyes, Vicar of St. Mary's, Kilburn, Thiepval, July 1-16.

Noyes, Capt. Talbot Ronald Arthur Herbert, Northumberland Fusiliers, Rev. Frederick Robert Halsey Herbert Noyes, Vicar of Dunnington, Somme, July 11-16.

Nunneley, Lt. Charles Francis, Northumberland Fusiliers, Rev. F. B. Nunneley, Vicar of Rennington, Neuve Chapelle, Oct. 26-14.

Nenneley, Major George Paterson, M.C., Bedford Regt., Rev. Frederick Barham Nunneley, Vicar of Rennington March 27-18.

Oakeley, Lt. Francis Eckley, R.N., Rev. James Oakeley, Vicar of Holy Trinity, Hereford, Lost in Submarine, Nov. -14.

Oakes, Arthur Wellesley, Australian I.F., Archdeacon of Bathurst, Rector of Kelso, N.S.W., Gallipoli, Aug. 7-15.

Odell, Lt. Robert Eric, Black Watch, Rev. Robert William Odell, Vicar of St. Mathew's, Brighton, Arras, Dec. 20-16.

Oldfield, Capt. Edmund George William, Manchester Regt., Rev, Edmund Oldfield, Vicar of Reddish, Gallipoli, June 5.15.

Oldham, Midshipman Cecil Henry, R.N., Rev. Egerton Haslope Oldham, Rector of Stanford on Teme, H.M.S. Vanguard, July 9-17.

Oldham, 2d. Lt. Llewellyn Haslope, Worcester Regt., Rev. Egerton Haslope Oldham, Rector of Stanford on Teme, Hulloch, Sept. 26-15.

Oliver, Capt. Cyril Francis Harrison, West Yorkshire Regt., Rev. Henry Francis Oliver, Vicar of Fenny Stratford, La Bassee, July 14-16.

Olivier, 2d. Lt. Jasper George, Duke of Cornwall's L.I., Rev. Henry Eden Olivier, Vicar of St. James', Croydon, Les Boeufs, Sept. 16-16.

Olivier, Capt. Robert Harold, Duke of Cornwall's L.I., Canon Olivier, of Salisbury, Rector of Wilton, Aisne, Sept. -14.

Olphert, 2d. Lt. Hugh Montgomery Archdale, Royal Munster Fusiliers, Rev. John Olphert, Rector of Umey, Londonderry, Somme, Sept. 9-16.

Ommaney, 2d. Lt. Alfred Erasmus Stuart, The Buffs, Rev. Erasmus Austin Ommaney, Vicar of St. Michael's, Portsmouth, Gwendecourt, Oct. 7-16.

Onslow, 2d. Lt. Thomas, Shropshire L.L, Rev. Matthew Richard Septimus Onslow, Rector of Stoke Edith, Arras, Jan, 6-17.

Orford, 2d. Lt. Stephen Mewburn, K.R.R.C., Canon Orford, of Bloemfontein, Ypres, Jan. 25-16.

Orpen, Lt. Walter Selwyn, Lancashire Fusiliers, Rev. John Herbert Orpen, Rector of Melton, Somme, July 6-16.

Orton, Major Cecil Alfred, R.G.A., Order of St. Stanislas, Rev. Francis Orton, Rector of Swyre, Reading, Sept. 30-18.

Osborne, Lt. Harold John, Hampshire Regt., Rev. George Edward Caulfield Osborne, Rector of Botley, Basra, Aug. 4-15.

Overton, Lt. Thomas Darwin, Lincoln Regt., Rev. Frederick Arnold Overton, Rector of East Barnet, Gallipoli, July 30-15.

Owen, Edward Austin Cowley, Canadian E.F., Rev. Arthur Frank Cowley Owen, Vicar of Pembury, Aug. 17- .

Owen, Lt. Arthur Edmund, Northants Regt., Rev. Arthur Frank Cowley Owen, Vicar of Pembury, Melville, Oct. 18-16.

Owen, Lt. John Latimer, Canadian E.F., Rev. John Robert Blayney Owen, Rector of Bradwell on Sea, Lille, Nov. 2-18.

Owen, 2d. Lt. Norman Moore, R.F.A., Rev. Octavius Edward Owen, Rector of Over Wallop, Chasseney, Sept. 13-14.

Owen, 2d. Lt. Philip Charles, Shropshire L.I., Rev. Loftus Meade Owen, Rector of Stockton, Bellewarde, Sept. 25-15.

Owen, Major Reginald Mansfield, Oxford & Bucks L.I., Dean of Ripon, Guillimont, Aug. 2-16.

Owen, Francis Whitwell, Royal Fusiliers, Rev. Edward Charles Everard Owen, Rector of Bucknell, Vermelles, March 31-16.

Oxland, Lt. Nowell, Border Regt., Rev. William Oxland, Vicar of Alston, Gallipoli, Aug. 10-15.

Packard, 2d. Lt. Walter Herbert, Suffolk Regt., Rev. Osborne Burgess Packard, of Depden, Somme, July 15-16.

Paget, Capt. Samuel James, Norfolk Regt., Bishop of Chester, Framerville, March 26-18.

Paget, 2d. Lt. John Christopher, R.G.A., Rev. Cecil George Paget, Rector of Stock Gayland, Apr. 26-17.

Paget, 2d. Lt. Michael Theodore, Lancashire Fusiliers, Rev. Cecil George Paget, Rector of Stock Gayland, Aug. 17-17.

Paget, Francis Austen Elliott, Royal Fusiliers, Rev. Cecil George Paget, Rector of Stock Gayland, Delville Wood, July 31-16.

Palmer, Lt.-Col. Cecil Howard, Warwickshire Regt., Rev. James Howard Palmer, Vicar of East Worldham, Gallipoli, July 25-15.

Palmer, Lt. Reginald John Allen, Wilts Regt., Rev. Edward John Palmer, Rector of Widmerpool, Amiens, July 22-16.

Palmes, Lt. Guy Nicholas, Yorkshire L.I., Rev. George Palmes, Vicar of Naburn, Ypres, May 8-15.

Panes, Arthur Benjamin, S.S. Malda, Rev. John Benjamin Panes, Rector of Torver, At Sea, Aug. 25-17.

Panes, 2d. Lt. Ernest Philip Morris, K.R.R.C., Rev. John Benjamin Panes, Rector of Torver, Ypres, Sept. 25-15.

Papprill, Capt. Frederick Ernest, East Lancashire Regt., Canon Frederick Papprill, Vicar of Holy Trinity, Leicester, Bapaume, June 3-17.

Paramore, Lt. Robert Edward Pynsent, Devonshire Regt., Rev. Joseph Rawle Paramore, Rector of Iddesleigh, Somme, July 28-16.

Park, Capt. James Wilfrid Haynes, Mentioned in Despatches, 22nd Cavalry I.A., Rev. James Park, Rector of Gosforth, Hai, Mesopotamia, Jan. 17-17.

Park, George Allan, R.A.F., Rev. George Edward Park, Vicar of Burton Fleming, Nancy Oct. 19-18.

Parker, Rev. Herbert Wallis Parker, Vicar of Docking.

Parker, Capt. Basil Stewart, Hampshire Regt., Rev. George Parker, Rector of Quainton, Gallipoli, Aug. 0-15.

Parker, Capt. Cecil William Hannington, R. Warwickshire Regt., Rev. William Henry Parker, Vicar of St. Peter's, Birmingham, Bazentin le Petit, Dec. 27-16.

Parker, Frederick John Bush, Coldstream Guards, Rev. Frederick Talbot Parker, Vicar of Knowle, Givenchy, Aug. 8-15.

Parmiter, George Geoffrey, R.A.S.C., Rev. George Parmiter, Vicar of Dawley Parva, Masasi, E. Africa, Jan. 11-18.

Parr, Lt. Hugh Wharton Myddleton, South Staffordshire Regt., Rev. Robert Heming Parr, of Scarborough, France, May 15-15.

Parsons, Capt. Alfred Henry, 9th Gurkhas, Rev. A. Parsons, Kut, March 8-16.

Partington, Capt. John Bertram, Devonshire Regt., Rev. Thomas Partington, Vicar of Netherfield, Tigris, Nov. 3-17.

Partridge, Capt. Robert Charles, 5th Dragoon Guards, Rev. William Adolphus Partridge, of Norwich,

Pascoe, 2d. Lt. Frank Guy Buckingham, Royal Irish Fusiliers, Rev. Frank Pascoe, Vicar of St. George's, Millom, Cumberland, Ypres, July 2-17.

Pater, 2d. Lt. Hugh, West Yorkshire Regt., Rev. Septimus Pater, Vicar of Sunderland, Scampton, Apr. 17-17.

Pattison, 2d. Lt. Charles Joseph, South African E.F., Rev. Joseph Pattison, Rector of Southwell, South Africa, Rouen, Oct. 17-16.

Pattison, Victor Reginald, South African E.F., Rev. Joseph Pattison, Rector of Southwell, South Africa, Delville Wood, July 16-16.

Paynter, Lt. Charles Theodore, R.N., Rev. Francis Samuel Paynter, Rector of Springfield, Zeebrugge, Apr. 23-18.

Payton, Lt. Clement, R.A.F., D.F.C., Belgian Croix de Guerre, Rev. Joseph Wattson Payton, Vicar of Calton, Lendelede, Oct. 2-18.

Payton, Frederick Thomas Croydon, R.E., Rev. Joseph Wattson Payton, Vicar of Calton, Somme, July 1-16.

Pearce, Lt. Maurice Leonard, R. Sussex Regt., Rev. Duncan Pearce, Vicar of Lynchmere, Palestine, Sept. 24-16.

Pearson, Capt. Alfred Christopher, Royal Warwicks, Bishop of Burnley, Kurdistan, Apr. 4-19.

Pearson, Lt. Charles Hugh, South Staffordshire Regt., Rev. Charles William Pearson, Vicar of Oker Hill, Vimy, March 19-16.

Pell, Lt.-Col. Beauchamp Tyndale, D.S.O., West Surrey Regt., Rev. Beauchamp Henry St. John Pell, Rector of Ickenham, Werwick, Nov. 4-14.

Pell, Major Albert Julian, Suffolk Regt., Rev. Beauchamp Henry St. John Pell, Rector of Ickenham, Tattenhall, Aug. 28-16.

Pelton, 2d. Lt. Kenneth Kemble, M.C., Leinster Regt., Rev. William Frederick Pelton, Vicar of Ullenhall, Ypres, Aug. 1-17.

Pemberton, Capt. Francis Percy Campbell, Life Guards, Canon Pemberton, of Trumptington, Moorslede, Oct. 19-14.

Penrose, Capt. Edward John McNiell, Mentioned in Despatches, R. Irish Fusiliers, Rev. John Trevenen Penrose, Rector of Petworth, Apr. 15- .

Penty, Basil, Australian I.F., Rev. Robert Penty, Vicar of Taralga, N.S.W., Les Boeufs, Jan, 1-17.

Penty, Robert Eric, Australian I.F., Rev. Robert Penty, Vicar of Taralga, N.S.W., Pozieres, July 28-16.

Pepys, Capt. Reginald Whitmore, Worcester Regt., Canon Pepys, Vicar of Hallow, Aisne, Sept. 21-14.

Percival, Lt.-Col. Arthur Jex Blake, Northumberland Fusiliers, Bishop of Hereford, Hooge, Oct. 31-14.

Peregrine, Lt. John Pryor Puxon, East Yorkshire Regt., Rev. David Wilkie Peregrine, Rector of Branstone-by-Belvoir, Somme, July 1-16.

Perry, Lt. Stephen Ralph, K.R.R.C., Rev. S. E. Perry, Guinchy, Sept. 17-16.

Peters, 2d. Lt. Gerard, Gloucester, Rev. Edward Peters, Vicar of Bishop Wilton, Chaulmes, Feb. 24-18.

Phillips, Rev. Edward Stanley Phillips, Rector of Bow.

Phillips, 2d. Lt. Cecil Ivor, R.A.F., Rev. Egbert Ivor Allen Phillips, of Clifton College, Oct. 27-17.

Phillips, Lt. Cyril Gordon, South Wales Borderers, Rev. Thomas Phillips, Vicar of Kerry, Montgomery, Passchendale, Nov. 10-17.

Phillips, Capt. M. Mclain, R.A.M.C., Rev. Thomas Ceredig Phillips, of Crumlin, Mon. Flanders, Nov. 4-14.

Phillips, 2d. Lt. Walter Henry Sherburn, East Yorkshire Regt., Rev. Walter Phillips, Vicar of Skirlaugh, Ancre, Sept, 16-16.

Phillpotts, Lt. Fitzroy Charles, Gloucester Regt., Rev. Ernest Alfred Phillpotts, Rector of Stapleton, Aug. 9-18.

Philpott, Capt. John Reginald, M.C., R.A.F., Canon John Nigel Philpott, Rector of Southchurch, Afion Kara Hissar, Jan. 15-18.

Phipps, Major Constantine James, R.E., D.S.O., M.C., Canon Phipps, of Aylesbury, Duren, Feb. 19-19.

Phipps, Lt. Charles Percy, Oxford & Bucks L.I., Canon Phipps, of Aylesbury, Lavantie, July 20-16.

Pickering, Lt. Basil Horace, The Buffs, Rev. Arthur Milner Pickering, Rector of Woolwich, Cologne, Dec. 1-15.

Pickop, James Taylor Greer, Royal Fusiliers, Canon Pickop, Vicar of Hatcliffe, London, June 21-17.

Pickop, Lt. William Bannister Augustus, Royal Fusiliers, Canon Pickop, Vicar of Hatcliffe, Rusnes, Oct. 24-18.

Pierson, 2d. Lt. Christopher Frank Kirshaw, R.A.F., Rev. Kirshaw Thomson Pierson, Vicar of Chertsey, Zuy-decoote, Oct. 10-17.

Pierssené, Lt. Frederick Andrew, Royal Sussex Regt., Rev. Rene Pierssené, Vicar of Chandler's Ford, Esquecberg, Sept. 6-18.

Pigott, Lt. Lancelot Botry, Hants Regt., Rev. Eversfield Botry Pigott, Rector of Ellisfield, Gallipoli, Aug. 6-15.

Pike, James Carey, Royal Lancaster Regt., Rev. James Kirk Pike, Vicar of St. Barnabas, Mossley Hill, Jouaixe, Sept. 8-14.

Pike, Clement Everard Gregory, Canadian E.F., Rev. James Kirk Pike, Vicar of St. Barnabas, Mossley Hill, Wulvergham, Feb. 6-16.

Pitts, 2d. Lt. Francis Burton, Leicester Regt., Canon Pitts, Rector of Loughborough, Bouchain, May 17-17.
Place, 2d. Lt. Philip Whitley, Northumberland Fusiliers, Rev. Ernest William Place, Rector of St. Barnabas, Cape Town, S.A., Aug. -18.
Platts, Capt. John Carrick, 17th Lancers, I.A., Rev. Charles Platts, Fellow of Trinity College, Cambridge, Mesopotamia, March 7-20.
Platts, Lt. Edgar Filmer Lovell, R.M.L.I., Rev. Charles Platts, Fellow of Trinity College, Cambridge, Ypres, Apr. 28-17.
Pleydell, Lt. John Marton Mansel, R.F.A., Canon Pleydell, of Sturminster-Newton, Sept. 22-10.
Plowman, Lt. Charles Hugh, Wilts Regt., Rev. Lionel Seymour Plowman, Rector of Ibberton, Doiran, Apr. 24-17.
Plummer, Lt. Arthur Henry, Liverpool Regt., Canon Plummer, of Liverpool, Festubert, May 17-15.
Plummer,
Polehampton, 2d. Lt. Frederick William, R.A.F., Rev. Edward Polehampton, Rector of Hartfield, Wady Debis, Apr. 26-15.
Ponsonby, Capt. Gerald Maurice, Inniskilling Fusiliers, Hon. & Rev. Maurice Ponsonby, of Wantage, Mons, Aug. 31-14.
Pope, Capt. Harold Edward, M.C., R.G.A., Rev. Arthur Frederick Pope, Vicar of Tring, Bazonvillers, Aug. 23-18.
Popham, Lt.-Com. Arthur Leybourne, R.N., Rev. E. Leybourne Popham, Vicar of Hemyoek, North Atlantic, Feb. 3-15.
Powell, 2d. Lt. Alban Wentworth, Queen's West Surrey, D.C.M., Rev. Arthur Wentworth Powell, Vicar of Minley, Somme, Aug. 21-16.
Powell, Capt. Henry Mitchell, South Staffordshire Regt., Rev. Henry Powell, Vicar of Stanningfield, France, Dec. 9-14.
Powell, Major John Harold Slade, R.F.A., Rev. John Powell, Rector of St. Clement's, Ipswich, Lille, Feb. 8-15.
Powell, Capt. Richard, R.F.A., Rev. George Bather Powell, Rector of Munslow, Le Treport, Aug. 22-17.
Powell, Lt. Robert Real, South Lancashires, Rev. John Real Powell, Rector of Armitage, Thiepval, Oct. 4-16.
Powell, Capt. Townsend George, Northants Regt., Rev. Townsend Powell, Vicar of Quinton, May 11-15.
Powell, Capt. Wilfred Roderick, Dorset Regt., Rev. Morgan Powell, Vicar of Aberaman, Wady Debis, Apr. 9-18.
Prangley, 2d. Lt. Charles Dean, Lincolnshire Regt., Rev. Charles Wilton Prangley, Rector of Bexwell, Flers, Sept. 25-16.
Price, 2d. Lt. Reginald, Warwickshire Regt., Rev. Thomas Price, Vicar of Claverdon, Somme, July 1-16.
Prichard, Lt. Frederick Giles, East Yorkshire Regt., Rev. Charles Collwyn Prichard, Vicar of Alresford, London, Aug. 9-15.
Prichard, Lt. Rowland George, Suffolk Regt., Rev. Charles Collwyn Prichard, Rector of Alresford, St. Julien, Apr. 27-15.
Prichard, Capt. Thomas Lewes, Royal Welsh Fusiliers, Rev. Thomas Prichard, Vicar of Amlwch, Boulogne, Nov. 9-14.
Prickard, 2d. Lt. Gerald Thornton, South Wales Borderers, Rev. William Edward Prickard, of Dderw, Gallipoli, June 4-14.
Priestley, Lt.-Col. Percival Thomas, R.A.M.C., Rev. Thomas Priestley, Vicar of Albrighton, Salonika, Sept. 28-18.
Prince, Lt. John Cecil Butler, London Regt., Rev. John Henry Prince, Vicar of Braunton, Souchy, Sept. 27-18.
Pritchard, Lt. Thomas L., Royal Welsh Fusiliers, Rev. T. Pritchard, Vicar of Llanbadrig, Anglesea, Nov. 9-14
Proctor, Lt. William Howard, D.S.O., Loyal North Lancashires, Rev. William George Proctor, of Jubbulpore, Gavrelle, Apr. 12-17.
Puckridge, Capt. Christopher Francis Hewitt, Duke of Cornwall's L.I., Rev. Oliver Puckridge, Vicar of Pinhoc, Ruyaulcowit, March 28-17.
Pulling, 2d. Lt. Oswald Langley, R.G.A., Rev. Edward Herbert Pulling, C.B.E., C.F., Loos Sept. 26-15.
Punchard, Capt. Alfred, North Staffordshire Regt., Mentioned in Despatches, Canon Punchard, of Ely, Baghdad, March 29-17, Ruyall.
Punchard, Lt. Edmund Elgood, Bedfordshire Regt., Canon Punchard, of Ely, Zandervoorde, Oct. 31-14.

Quin, Walter William Macgregor, Royal Dublin Fusiliers, Rev. William Quin, Rector of Finvoy, Co. Antrim, Boulogne, June 22-18.
Quinn, Rev. William Trevor Quinn, Vicar of Cudworth.

Raban, Lt.-Col. R. B. C., Royal Scots, Rev. George Ferguson Cockburn Raban, Vicar of Bishop's, Hull, May 11-16.
Radcliffe, 2d. Lt. William Yonge, Wilts Regt., Rev. Arthur Caynton Radcliffe, Rector of Rockbourne, Gallipoli, Aug. 15-15.
Raikes, 2d. Lt. John Francis, Essex Regt., Rev. Thomas Digby Raikes, Rector of Whichford, Flers, Oct. 10-16.
Railton, Lt. Geoffrey Lancelot, R.A.N.S., Rev. William Railton, Vicar of Plumpton, Farnborough, Sept. 12-16.
Ram, 2d. Lt. Percival John, Manchester Regt., Rev. Stephen Adye Scott Ram, Vicar of St. Mary's, Hull, Somme, July 1-16.
Ramsbottom, Lt. Basil William, Norfolk Yeomanry, Rev. William Henry Ramsbottom, Vicar of Lacock, Hazebrouck, Aug. 19-18.
Ratliff, Capt. Edward Francis, M.C., Rifle Brigade, Rev. Frank Howe Ratliff, Rector of Moccas, Passchendale, Dec. 2-17.

Raynes, Lt. Arthur Herbert, Essex Regt., Rev. Herbert Alfred Raynes, Vicar of St. Saviour's, Nottingham, Loos, Sept. 26-15.

Raynor, 2d. Lt. Harold Arthur Livingston, Rifle Brigade, Rev. Arthur Guy Sandars Raynor, Vicar of Steventon, London, June 7-18.

Rayson, Capt. William Humphrey Ronald, R.F.A., Rev. William Robert Rayson, Vicar of Coatham, Essigny le Grand, March 27-18.

Reade, 2d. Lt. Charlton Leverton Ridout, Sussex Regt., Rev. Edward Frank Reade, of Brighton, Sept. 9-16.

Reed, Capt. Andrew Gordon, Royal Welsh Fusiliers, Rev. Samuel Reed, Rector of Llangyniew, Gallipoli, Aug. 10-15.

Rees, 2d. Lt. Kenneth David Rees, Cheshire Regt., Rev. John Francis Rees, Rector of Halkyn, Calais, Aug. 29-17.

Rees, 2d. Lt. David Melvyn, Durham L.I., Rev. J. Rees, Apr. 12-17.

Rennard, Capt. Edward Marmaduke, North Lancashire Regt., Rev. David Smith Rennard, Vicar of Heapy, Albert, Aug. 8-16.

Richards, Lt. Hugh Liddon, New Zealand E.F., Bishop of Dunedin, N.Z., Gallipoli, May 4-15.

Richards, Lt. Robert, New Zealand E.F., Bishop of Dunedin, Alexandria, May 23-15.

Richards, 2d. Lt. Julian David Eaton, Sussex Regt., Rev. John Francis Richards, Rector of South Luffenham, Loos, Sept. 25-15.

Richards, Capt. Walter Hayes Pickering, Rev. R. E. Richards, Rector of Little Heaton, Gallipoli, May 10-15.

Richardson, 2d. Lt. Rodney Francis, Manchester Regt., Rev. Mark Richardson, Vicar of St. John's, Huddersfield, Sanctuary Wood, July 31-17.

Richardson, Lt. Richard Francis, Warwickshire Regt., Mentioned in Despatches, Rev. Edward Taswell Richardson, Vicar of Moreton Morrell, Rouen, Sept. 30-15.

Richardson, Capt. Edric Hugh Barnsley, Wilts Regt., Rev. Albert Thomas Richardson, Vicar of Bradford on Avon, Givenchy, June 15-15.

Richardson, 2d. Lt. Samuel George, R.F.A., Rev. George Frederick Richardson, Rector of St. Peter, York, Oxford, Feb. 28-21.

Richardson, Lt. Francis Aylmer, R.F.A., Rev. Francis Richardson, of Carbridge on Tyne, Chemin des Dames, May 27-18.

Richardson, Capt. George Hugh, Manchester Regt., Rev. William Richardson, Vicar of Poulton le Fylde, Lezzo, Italy, Oct. 29-18.

Richardson, Lt. Maurice Lewis George, South Lancashire Regt., Rev. Lewis Richardson, of Binley, Baincourt, Feb. 28-17.

Rickards, Lt. Hew Wardrop Brooke, R.F.A., Rev. Walter Brooke Richards, Rector of Nettleton, Wielsbeke, July 28-17.

Riddle, 2d. Lt. Francis Edmund Langton, Oxford & Bucks L.I., Rev. Arthur Esmond Riddle, Rector of Tadmarton, Richebourg St. Avoue, May 16-15.

Ridsdale, Robert Hugh, Canadian E.F., Rev. Charles Joseph Ridsdale, Vicar of St. Peter's, Folkestone, Ypres, June 2-16.

Rigby, 2d. Lt. James Richard Anderton, Yorkshire Regt., Rev James Rigby, Vicar of Sheriff Hutton, La Bassee, Sept. 26-15.

Roberts, 2d. Lt. Francis, R. Fusiliers, Canon Roberts, Rector of Longsight, Les Boeufs, Oct. 27-16.

Roberts, Capt. Cecil Llewellyn Norton, R. Warwickshire Regt., Rev. Albert Pryor Roberts, Vicar of St. Margaret's, Birmingham, Polygon Wood, Oct. 9-17.

Roberts, 2d. Lt. Frederick Leslie Barry, 2d Rajputs, Rev. Francis Barry Roberts, Vicar of Bettisfield, Aden, Dec. 22-17.

Roberts, Laurence Guy Hough, R.N.D.S., Rev. Albert Pryor Roberts, Vicar of St. Margaret's, Birmingham, Gallipoli, July 21-15.

Roberts, 2d. Lt. Noel Humphreys, King's Own Shropshires, Rev. Frederick Roberts, Vicar of St. Giles', Shrewsbury, Monchy, Apr. 32-17.

Roberts, 2d. Lt. Philip Hugh Gore, Gordon Highlanders, Rev. William Walter Roberts, of Fensington, Bellincourt, Aug. 21-15.

Robertson, Lt. Ernest Cecil Lennox, London Regt., Rev. Arthur George Lennox Robertson, of St. Stephen's, Lewisham, Loos, Oct. 18-15.

Robertson, Lt. George Hawthorne Minot, Nigeria Regt., Rev. George Philip Robertson, of Sandhead, Sandhead, March 10-19.

Robinson, Lt. Charles Arthur, Royal Inniskilling Fusiliers, Canon Robinson, of Ardess, Co. Fermanagh, Monchy, Apr. 9-17.

Robinson, Capt. Edmond, R.A.M.C., Rev. Edmond Robinson, Vicar of Glenageary, Co. Dublin, Arras, March 20-17.

Robinson, Capt. Leslie John, Northants Regt., Rev. William Robinson, Vicar of East Haddon, Neuve Chappelle, Apr. 12-15.

Robinson, Sub.-Lt. Richard Arthur Wynne, R.N.V.R., Rev. Andrew Craig Robinson, Rector of Ballymoney, Cork, Albert, Feb. 2-17.

Rodgerson, Lt. James Stuart, Canadian E.F., Rev. William Patrick Rodgerson, Lens, May 13-17.

Roe, 2d. Lt. Cyril Charles, R.M.L.I., Canon Gordon Roe, Rector of Blakeney, Oppy Wood, Apr. 28-17.

Rogers, Major Wilfrid Frank, D.S.O., R.F.A., Rev. Alfred George Rogers, Rector of Gatton, Arras, May 19-17.

Rogerson, John Hamilton, K.R.R.C., Rev. George Rogerson, Vicar of Peak Forest, Fulham, Nov. 15-16.

Rolfe, George Somerville, Canon Rolfe, Rector of Kirk Bramwith, Lusitania, May 7-16.

Rooke, C K J, Tasmanian Regt., Canon Rooke, of Salisbury.

Rose, Capt. Eric Wollaston, Mentioned in Despatches, London Rifles, Rev. Percy Wollaston Rose, Vicar of Norton-by-Daventry, Gavrelle, March 28-18.

Roseveare, 2d. Lt. Harold William, Wilts Regt. Rev. Richard Polgreen Roseveare, Vicar of Lewisham, Vailly Sept. 20-14.

Roseveare, Lt. Francis Bernard, Scinde Rifles, Rev. Richard Polgreen Roseveare, Vicar of Lewisham, Samarra, Nov. 9-17.

Rosling, Capt. Charles Holbrook, Duke of Cornwall's L.I., Rev. Charles Douglas Rosling, Rector of Caerhays, Selle, Oct. 22-18.

Round, Capt. William Haldane, Sherwood Foresters, Rev. William Round, Vicar of East Drayton, Gounincourt, July 1-16.

Rowley, 2d. Lt. Walter Austin, Leicestershire Regt., Rev. Walter Poutney Rowley, Rector of Theydon Garnon, Arras, July 17-17.

Roy, Capt. Kenneth James, Middlesex Regt., Rev. James Roy, Rector of Stockton on Forest, Mons, Aug. 23-14.

Royds, Lt. Thomas Alington, R.A.F., Rev. Nathaniel Royds, Rector of Little Barford, Toulincourt, Apr. 20-18.

Rudall, 2d. Lt. Bertram Allen, West Kent Regt., Rev. John Bertram Rudall, Vicar of St. Jude's, Southwark, Monchy, July 17-17.

Rudd, Capt. Kenneth Sutherland, West Yorkshire Regt., Prebendary Eric John Sutherland Rudd, Rector of Souldern, Inchy, Oct. 10-18.

Ruddock, Henry Mark, Canadian E.F., Rev. Mark Ernest Ruddock, Vicar of Ardeley, Courcelette, Sept. 15-16.

Ruddock, Edward Oliver, N.Z.E.F., Rev. David Ruddock, Archdeacon of Hawkes Bay, N.Z., Gallipoli, May 11-15.

Ruddock, Capt. Walter David, N.Z.E.F., Rev. David Ruddock, Archdeacon of Hawkes Bay, N.Z., France, June 13-17.

Ruegg, Lt. Kenneth Stanes, Sherwood Foresters, Rev. Ferdinand Stanes Ruegg, Rector of Wetherden, Aisne, Sept. 20-14.

Russell, Lt.-Col. James Cosmo, D.S.O., Mentioned in Despatches, Rev. Henry Charles Russell, Rector of Wollaton, Ypres, July 31-17.

Russell, Lt. Francis Wycliffe, M.C., Queen's Westminster Rifles, Canon Alfred Francis Russell, Rector of Chingford, Aug. 27-18.

Rust, Edward, Yorkshire Regt., Rev. Edward Rust, Vicar of Hamsteels, St. Julien, Apr. 29-15.

Ryan, Lt. Alexander Charles Thomas, Middlesex Regt., Rev Alexander Solomon Kroenig Ryan, Vicar of Parkeston, Englefontaine, Oct. 28-18.

Salmon, 2d. Lt. Bernard Bryant, M.C., Manchester Regt., Rev. William Bryant Salmon, Rector of Stoke Newington, Trones Wood, July 9-16.

Salmon, Lt. Cecil Gordon, Sherwood Foresters, Rev. A. Salmon, of Burmah, Ypres, June 13-15.

Salusbury, 2d. Lt. Norman Horace Pemberton, Border Regt., Rev. Norman Salusbury, Rector of St. Chad's, Lichfield, Gallipoli, Dec. 1-15.

Samson, Capt. Arthur Legge, M.C., Royal Welsh Fusiliers, Rev. Edward Samson, Rector of Armitage, Loos, Sept. 25-15.

Sanctuary, Capt. Charles Lloyd, M.C., Suffolk Regt., Rev. Charles Lloyd Sanctuary, Vicar of Frampton, Boulogne, Nov. 15-16.

Sandbach, Major William, Lancaster Regt., Rev. Gilbert Sandbach, Rector of Upper Sapey, Gallipoli, Aug. 9-15.

Sandford, Capt. Folliott Clement Richard, M.C., K.O. Yorkshire L.I., Archdeacon of Doncaster, La Bassee, Feb. 22-17.

Sands, Capt Leslie Kelham, Lancashire Fusiliers, Rev. Hubert Sands, Vicar of Burbage, Canon of Birmingham, Ypres, Apr. 28-16.

Sangar, Walter Augustine, Royal Fusiliers, Rev. James Mortimer Sanger, Rector of Elworthy, Bailleul, Oct. 2-17.

Sant, Lt. Edward Medley, R.A.F., Rev. Edward Sant, Vicar of Elsenham, Ypres, Sept. 1-17.

Sargent, Lt. Reginald Fitzgerald, Royal Irish Regt., Rev. John Fitzgerald Sargent, of Seaford, Polygon Wood, Oct. 5-17.

Saulez, Major Arthur Travers, R.F.,A. Rev. Robert Travers Saulez, Rector of Willingale Doe, Arras, Apr. 22-17.

Saulez, Capt. Alfred Gordon, R.A.S.C., Rev. Robert Travers Saulez, Rector of Willingale Doe, Baghdad, July 5-21.

Saunders, Capt. Noel Martyn, Mentioned in Despatches, Border Regt., Rev. Clement Morgan Saunders, Rector of Rumboldswyke, Amerval, Oct. 20-18.

Saunderson, Lt. Robert de Bedick, West African Force, Rev. Robert de Bedick Saunderson of Milton, Kent, Lukuledi, Oct. 18-17.

Savage, Lt. Cuthbert Farrar, Northumberland Fusiliers, Canon Savage, of Hexham, Popperinghe, June 20-17.

Savage, Capt. John Ardkeen, Northants Regt., Rev. Francis Forbes Savage, Vicar of Flushing, Troyon, Sept. 17-14.

Savatard, Major Thomas Warner, Manchester Regt., Rev. Louis Savatard, Vicar of Holy Trinity, Darwen. Gallipoli, May 29-15.

Schofield, Edwin Borwick, R.F.A., Rev. Daniel Schofield, Vicar of Stalmine, La Bassee, Oct. 16-18.

Schooling, Rev. Cecil Herbert, C.F., Rev. Frederick Schooling, Dickebosch, June 21-17.

Scott, Geoffrey Lawrence, South African Scottish, Rev. Inglis Charles Reymond Scott, Vicar of Chute, Delville Wood, July 15-16.

Scott, Edward Grigor, Argyll & Sutherland Highlanders, Rev. William Scott of Morstowle, Epernay, July 23-18.

Scott, Kenneth,

Scott, Henry Hutton, Canadian E.F., Rev. Frederick George Scott, Rector of St. Matthew's, Quebec, Somme, Oct. 21-10.

Scott, Lt. Richard Thomas Folliott, East Yorkshire Regt., Rev. Richard Curtis Folliott Scott, Rector of Hulcote, Armentieres, March 16-15.

Scott, 2d. Lt. John Hastings Folliott, Oxford & Bucks LX, Rev. Richard Curtis Folliott Scott, Rector of Hulcote, Arras, Apr. 9-17,

Scott, 2d. Lt. Robert Walter Theodore Gordon, Seaforth Highlanders, Rev. Robert Scott, of Wilson College, Bombay, London, Aug. 15-16.

Scott, Capt. Samuel Geoffrey, R.A.M.C., Rev. Samuel Gilbert Scott, Rector of Havant, Istrana, Italy, Jan. 6-18.

Scott, Thomas Henry, Royal Scots, Rev. William Frank Scott, Roeux, Apr. 28-17,

Searight, Lt. Gerald Graves, R. Dublin Fusiliers, Rev. Frederic Sidney Searight, of Wandsworth, Basra, Nov. 12-20.

Seaton, Capt. Alexander Adam, Fellow of Pembroke College, Cambridge, Cambridgeshire Regt., Rev. John Abdiel Seaton, Vicar of St. John's, Clechkeaton, Armentieres, Sept. 4-15.

Sellar, 2d. Lt. James Arthur, Oxford & Bucks L.L, Rev. J. A. Sellar, Bapaume, Apr. 3-17.

Selwyn, Capt. Christopher Wakefield, Leicester Regt., Rev. Edward Carus Selwyn, of Uppingham, Bailleul, May 19-15.

Selwyn, Lt. Arthur Penrose, R.A.F., Rev. Edward Carus Selwyn, of Uppingham, Gosport, May 18-16.

Selwyn, Lt. George Vincent Carus, R.A., Rev. Edward Carus Selwyn, of Uppingham, Rouen, Oct. 25-18.

Sewart, Lt. Gerald Evelyn Shuldham, Bengal Lancers, Rev. Anthony Wilkinson Sewart, Rector of Brignall, Arras, May 8-16.

Seymour, Lt. Neville, R.N., Rev. Isaac Lothian Seymour, Vicar of Maldon, H.M.S. Queen Mary, Jutland, May 31-16.

Shann, Lt. Reginald Arthur, East Lancashire Regt., Rev. Reginald Shaun, Rector of Chenies, Hargicourt, March 21-15.

Sharland, Id. Charles Frederick, Australian I.F., Rev. Frederick Burnett Sharland, of Tasmania, Passchendale, Oct. 12-17.

Sharpe, 2d. Lt. Anthony Herbert, King's Liverpool Regt., Rev. William Robert Sharpe, Vicar of Little Barrington.

Sharpin, 2d. Lt. Frank Lloyd, Bedfordshire Regt., Archdeacon of Bombay, Somme, Oct. 14-16.

Sharpies, Capt. Evelyn Horace Guy, R.A.F., Rev. Henry Milner Sharpies, Rector of Finghall, Kent, Jan. 19-18.

Sharpies, Sub.-Lt. Thomas Henry Wilfrid, R.N., Rev. Henry Milner Sharpies, Rector of Finghall, H.M.S. Hampshire, June 5-16.

Shaw, Capt. Marmaduke Marshall, Sherwood Foresters, Rev. Marmaduke Spicer Shaw, Vicar of All Saint's, Exmouth, Lagnicourt, Mar. 2-18.

Shaw, Capt. Alexander James Macintosh, King's Own Scottish Borderers, Archdeacon Shaw, of Tokyo, Japan, July 1-16.

Shaw, Lt. Arthur Gilby, Sherwood Foresters, Bishop of Buckingham, Ypres, Dec. 24-15.

Shaw, Lt. Bernard Henry Gilbert, West Yorkshire Regt., Bishop of Buckingham, Neuve Chapelle, Dec. 19-14.

Shaw, Capt. Edward Arthur, Oxford & Bucks L.L, Bishop of Buckingham, Geudecourt, Oct. 7-16.

Shaw, 2d. Lt. Bernard Hudson, Cheshire Regt., Rev. George William Hudson Shaw. Rector of St. Botolph's, Bishopsgate, E. May 19-15.

Shaw, 2d. Lt. Edward Lockhart, West Surrey Regt., Rev. Charles Shaw, of St. Albans, Ovillers, Aug. 5-16.

Shaw, Lt.-Col. Robert Edward Frederic, London Regt., M.C., Mentioned in Despatches, Rev. Robert Villiers George Shaw, Vicar of Langlebury, Boisleux, Aug. 23-18.

Shaw, Lt. Giles Havergal, Bedfords, Rev. William Henry Shaw, Rector of Stapleton, Arras, April 10-17.

Shaw, Lt.-Col. Greville Havergal, C.E.F., Rev. William Henry Shaw, Rector of Stapleton, Valenciennes, Nov. 3-18.

Sheehan, Lt. Gordon Keith Patrick, Northants Regt., Rev. Thomas Moore Sheehan, Vicar of Temple Bruer, Aug. 28-18.

Sheepshanks, 2d. Lt. William, K.R.R.C., Bishop of Norwich, Nieuport, July 10-17.

Shegog, Capt. Richard Wellington, R.A.M.C., Rev. Richard William Ashe Shegog, Rector of Holmpatrick, Ypres, Aug. 1-17.

Shelton, Rev. Norman Wilfrid Shelton, Vicar of Littleport.

Shepherd, Alban Munn, Australian Imperial Force.

Shepherd, Lt. Edwin Alexander, M.G.C., Rev. Edwin Thomas Shepherd, Vicar of Longsleddale, Bethune, Apr. 13-18.

Shepherd, Douglas A. McKay, Queen's Westminster Rifles, Canon William Mutrie Shepherd, of Appleby, Leuze, Sept. 19-16.

Shields, Lt. Hugh John Sladen, R.A.M.C., Rev. Arthur John Shields, Rector of Thornford, Ypres, Oct. 27-14.

Shields, Capt. William Francis Waugh, Shropshire L.L, Rev. William Henry Shields, Rector of Hughley, Ypres, Sept. 25-15.

Shilcock, Lt. John Wynton, West Surrey Regt., Rev. Sidney Isaac, Welbank Shilcock Rector of Titsey, Ctesiphon, Nov. 23-15.

Shipley, 2d, Lt. Arthur Hammond Butler, Yorkshire Regt., Rev. Arthur Granville Shipley, Vicar of All Saints, Pontefract, Thiepval, Sept. 27-16.

Shore, Arthur John Mutton, Canadian E. F., Rev. Arthur Shore, Rector of Ilderton, Ontario, Passchendale, Nov. 11-17.

Shorland, John Maitland, Midshipman, R.N., Rev. Maitland Arthur Shorland, Rector of Church Lawford, H.M.S. Invincible, Jutland, May 31-16.

Short, Lt.-Col. William Ambrose, C.M.G., R.F.A., Rev. A. Short, Armentieres, June 21-17.

Shuttleworth, Lt. Kingsley Christopher, Suffolk Regt., Professor Henry Carey Shuttleworth, France, Nov. 19-17.

Silvester, 2d. Lt. Anson Lloyd, Sussex Regt., Rev. James Silvester, Vicar of Gt. Clacton, Cuichy, Dec. 31-14.

Simmonds, Percy Grenfell, King's Liverpool Regt., Rev. Delasaux Egginton Mount Simmonds, Vicar of St. Andrew's, Ramsbottom, Maricourt. June 27-16.

Simmonds, Aubrey Henry, R. Warwicks, Rev. Charles Simmonds, Vicar of Exhall, Denain, Oct. 24-18.

Simpson, Lt. Hugh Delafosse, K.R.R.C., Rev. Robert Henry Bridges Simpson, Vicar of Okewood, Ypres, Aug. 24-17.

Simpson, Capt. John Edmund, Yorkshire L.I., Rev. John Curwen Simpson, of Thurnscoe, Messines, Oct. 31-14.

Simpson, Lt. Stewart Basil, Canadian Mounted Rifles, Canon Simpson, of Charlottetown, Prince Edward's Island, Razine, Oct. 1-16.

Sketchley, Major Ernest Frederick Powys, D.S.O., R.M.L.I., Mentioned in Despatches, Rev. Ernest Powys Sketchley, of Exmouth, Serre, Oct. 12-16.

Skinner, Lt. Robert Leonard Grahame, R.A.F., Rev. Henry Leonard Skinner, Rector of Callander, N.B., Vielle Chapelle, May 3-18.

Skinner, Ronald Sweyn, London Regt., Rev. Frederick William Skinner, Vicar of Tiberham, Hill 60, Feb. 3-15.

Skinner, 2d. Lt. Edward Dudley, Manchester Regt., Rev. Ernest Edward Becher Skinner, Vicar of Chacombe, Ypres, Sept. 10-17.

Skyrme, 2d. Lt. Richard Edward Elcho, Wilts. Regt., Rev. Frank Elcho Skyrme, Vicar of Winterbourne Earls, Ploegsteert, Feb. 6-17.

Slater, G. R. V., R.N., Rev, Plymouth, Sept. 30-18

Slater, Lt. Gilbert John Leigh, Worcester Regt., Rev. Francis Slater of Godalming, France, Apr. 30-16.

Slater, Capt. Leonard, Sussex Regt., Rev. Francis Slater, of Godalming, Aisne, Sept. 14-14.

Slater, Walter Theodore, Canadian E.F., Rev. Henry Horrocks Slater, Rector of Thornhaugh, Lens, Aug. 15-17.

Slingsby, Midshipman John, R.N., Rev. Charles Slingsby, of Scriven Park, H.M.S. Formidable, Jan. 1-15.

Smart, Lt. Edward Treloar, R.A.F., Rev. John Raester Smart, Chaplain of Tonbridge School, Amiens, March 27-18.

Smith, 2d. Lt. A B, M.G.C., Sept. -15.

Smith, 2d. Lt. Arthur Charles Vaughan, East Yorkshire Regt., Rev. Walter Edmund Smith, Vicar of Andover, Poelchappelle, Oct. 9-17.

Smith, Lt. Humphry Walter, R.N., Rev. Walter Edward Smith, Vicar of Andover, Persian Gulf, Jan. 19-18.

Smith, Lt. Bernard Arthur Knights, Rifle Brigade, Rev. Leslie Knights Smith, Vicar of Uttoxeter, Laventie, Sept. 4-15.

Smith, Philip Arnold Knights, Rev. Leslie Knights Smith, Vicar of Uttoxeter, Died from injuries in training, Uttoxeter, Apr. 12-18.

Smith, Lt. Charles Francis Bateman, Suffolk Regt., Canon George Herbert Smith, of Madras, Ypres, Feb. 15-15.

Smith, Herbert Henry, Canadian E.F., Canon George Herbert Smith, Canon of Madras, Vimy Ridge, Apr. 12-17.

Smith, William Fishburn Donkin, Canadian E.F., Canon George Herbert Smith, Canon of Madras, Otterpool, Aug. 29-15.

Smith, Capt. Everard Cecil, Royal Fusiliers, Rev. Cecil Evan Smith, Rector of Titsey, Vimy, Aug. 24-15.

Smith, Lt. Frank Dawson, Oxford & Bucks L.I., Rev. Charles Clare Dawson Smith, Rector of Nash, Jubaland, Jan. 11-20.

Smith, James Henry Hattersley, Norfolk Regt., Rev. Percy Hattersley Smith, of Cheltenham College, Loos, Oct. 7-15.

Smith, Lt. Geoffrey Alban Hattersley, R.N., H.M.S. Lark, Rev. Percy Hattersley Smith, of Cheltenham College, Devonport, Nov. 1-15.

Smith, Lt. John Kenneth Brice, Lincolnshire Regt., Rev. Brice Smith, Rector of Hameringham, Ypres, Sept. 11-15.

Smith, Lt. Martin Kirke, R.F.A., Rev. Arnold Kirke Smith, Rector of Boxworth, Fricourt, Dec. 14-15.

Smith, 2d. Lt. Thomas Sydney, Dorsetshire Regt., Rev. Sydney Edward Smith, Rector of Sprotborough, Le Bassee, Oct. 13-14.

Smith, Lt. William Gerald Furness, North Staffordshire Regt., Rev. George Furness Smith, Rector of Kedleston, Ypres, July 5-15.

Smith, 2d. Lt. William Woodthorpe Barnard, R.F.A., Rev Barnard Gooch Barnard Smith, Rector of North Cove, Somme, Oct. 21-16.

Snowden, Lt. Harcourt John, Hertfordshire Regt., Rev. Harcourt Charles Vaux Snowden, Vicar of St. Peter's, Broadstairs, Richebuorg, St. Avoue, Jan. 11-15.

Snowden, Capt. Henry Frederick, London Regt., Rev. Richard Kemphay Snowden, Vicar of Ledsham, Somme, Oct. 6-16.

Soames, Major Alfred, D.S.O., E. Kent Regt., Rev. Gordon Soames, Rector of Mildenhall, Hulloch, Oct. 13-15.

Somerset, Capt. Noel Henry Plantagenet, A.S.C., Rev. Henry Plantagenet Somerset, Rector of Crickhowell, Upham, Sept. 7-21,

Soole, Seymour Waldegrave, R.F.A., Rev. Seymour Henry Soole, Vicar of Greyfriars, Reading, Reading, Feb. 3-17,

Sorby, 2d. Lt. Charles Malin Clifton, Monmouthshire Regt., Rev. Albert Ernest Sorby, Rector of Darfield, Ypres, May 8-15.

Southwell, Lt. Evelyn Herbert Lightfoot, Rifle Brigade, Canon Southwell, of Worcester, Les Boeufs, Sept. 15- .

Southwell, Lt. Henry Kenneth, R.N., Bishop of Lewes, Baltic, Submarine L55, June 3-19.

Speke, Rev. Hugh, Lancashire Fusiliers, Rev. Benjamin Speke, Rector of Dowlish Wake, Vierstat, Aug. 11-15.

Spencer, Lt. Edmond, Wilts Regt., Rev. William Edmund Spencer, Vicar of St. Botolph's, Colchester, Ypres, Oct. 24-14.

Spencer, Edwin Pelham, Australian I.F., Archdeacon of Young, N.S.W., Noreuil, May 5-17.

Spens, Andrew Nathaniel Wadham, Essex Regt., Archdeacon of Lahore.

Spink, Capt. Eric Minor, North Staffordshire Regt., Rev. Edmund Spink, Vicar of Bakewell, Baku, Sept. 14-18.

Sprigg, Capt. Henry Aldwin Guildford, Hampshire Regt., Rev. Herbert Guildford Sprigg, Rector of Emsworth, Palestine, May 9-18.

Sprott, Capt. Maurice William Campbell, M.C., Norfolk Regt., Bishop of Wellington, N.Z., Lagnicourt, March 21-18.

Spurling, Capt. Francis Eyton, Rifle Brigade, Canon Frederick William Spurling, of Chester, Poperinghe, Dec. 6-17.

Squire, Lt. Stanley Charles, Gloucester Regt., Rev. Charles Henry Squire, Vicar of Southrop, Gallipoli, Aug. 9-15.

Squires, Capt. Francis Chavasse, 23rd Sikhs, Rev. Henry Charles Squires, Vicar of Holy Trinity, Richmond, Aden, July 7-15.

Squires, Capt. Robert Dewar, Sherwood Foresters, Rev. Robert Alford Squires, Vicar of St. Peter's, St. Albans, Gallipoli, Aug. 7-15.

Stables, Lt. James Howard, Gurkha Rifles, Rev. Walter Howard Stables, Vicar of St. Chad's, Far Headingley, Sanna, Mesopotamia, Feb. 17-17.

Staley, Lt. Edward Vernon, R.F.A., Rev. Vernon Staley, Canon of Inverness, Rector of Ickford, Epehy, Sept. 18-18.

Stamper, 2d. Lt. Geoffrey Sidebotom Parker, Sherwood Foresters, Rev. William Parker Stamper, Vicar of Stonebroom, Somme, March 24-18.

Stamper, Hugh Gordon, Dublin Fusiliers, Rev. T. A. Stamper, of Monaline, France, Nov. 13-16.

Standage, Herbert Raymond, Royal Fusiliers, Rev. Samuel Ray Standage, Vicar of Gt. Bourton, Givenchy, May 17-16.

Standen, Capt. Leslie James Denman, Lincoln Regt., Canon Standen, Vicar of Gainsborough, Souchze, March 18-16.

Stansfield, Lt.-Col. John Raymond Evelyn, Gordon Highlanders, Rev. J. B. E. Stansfield, Rector of Downham, Sept. 28-15.

Stephenson, Lt.-Col. Ernest William Rokeby, Middlesex Regt., Rev. W. Stephenson, Ypres, Apr. 23-15.

Stevens, Lt. Henry Francis Binglow, West Kent Regt., Canon Stevens, of Rochester, Armentieres, Sept. 17-15.

Stewart, Rev. James Robert, C.F. (formerly of W. China), Rev. Robert W. Stewart, of C.M.S., Fuh Kien, China, Jan. -16.

Stidston, Capt. William Popkiss, Leinster Regt., Rev. Samuel Stidston, Vicar of Shaugh Prior, Poperinghe, Aug. 2-17.

Still, Frank Albert Willis, Canadian E.F., Rev. Thomas Allen Still, Rector of Kyre Wyard, Duisans, July 27-18.

Stitt, Lt. Innes D'Auvergne Stewart, Westminster Rifles, Rev. Samuel Stewart Stitt, Rector of Stretham, Arras, March 28-18.

Stocker, Hugh, N.Z.E.F., Rev. Harry Stocker, Archdeacon of Invergargill, N.Z., Messines.

Stocker, Lancelot, N.Z.E.F., Rev. Harry Stocker, Archdeacon of Invergargill, N.Z., La Plas Doure.

Stockley, Capt. Philip Lloyd, S. Staffordshire Regt., Rev. Joseph John Gabbett Stockley, Rector of Wolverhampton, Verbrandon, Molen, Apr. 26-18.

Stokes, Francis Herbert, Australian I.F., Rev. Francis Herbert Stokes, Rector of Chafers, South Australia, Gallipoli, Apr. 27-15.

Stone, Lt. Tom Pearce Griffith, R.F.A., Rev. Thomas Stone, Vicar of Barrow-on-Soar, Mesopotamia, Feb. 5-17.

Stones, Capt. G. L. Boys, Rev. George Boys Stones, Vicar of St. Thomas', Garstang.

Stonex, Lt. Francis Hugh Tilney, Dublin Fusiliers, Canon Stonex, of New Brighton, New Brighton, Feb. 1-18.

Storrs, Lt. Francis, R.N.V.R., Dean of Rochester, Nov. 10-18.

Stott, Edward Bleackley, R. Warwickshire Regt., Rev. James Augustine Stott, of Devizes, Newcastle-on-Tyne, Oct. 12-14.

Stratford, Lt. Laurence, Rifle Brigade, Rev. William Thomas Stratford, Vicar of Rillington, Fampoux, March 28-18.

Stuart, 2nd Lt. Maurice Stevenson, Rev. W. S. Stuart, of Glasgow, June 15-18.

Stubbs, 2d. Lt. William Norman, Cheshire Regt., Rev. Frederick William Stubbs, Vicar of Arbory, I.M., Solesmes, Oct. 29-18.

Sumner, Col. Charles Maunior, Devon Regt., Rev. John Maunior Sumner, Rector of Buriton, Morval, June 30-16.

Sunderland, Lt.-Col. Joseph Elton, Rev. James Sunderland, Vicar of Eggington, July 31-17.

Sutherland, George, Argyll & Sutherland Highlanders, Rev. George Sutherland of Aberdeen, Aubigny, June 17-18.

Sutton, Geoffrey Alfred, Irish Guards, Rev. Edwin Sutton, Vicar of Eaton Bray, Bourton Wood, Nov. 27-17.

Swallow, 2d. Lt. Hervey Launcelot St. George, York & Lancaster Regt., Rev. William Swallow, Rector of Weston Flavell, Loos, Sept. 26-15.

Sweet, Major John Hales, Canadian E.F., Archdeacon of Victoria, British Columbia, Vimy Apr. 9-17.

Sweet, Capt. Leonard Herbert, Hampshire Regt., Rev. Charles Francis Long Sweet, Rector of Symondsbury, France, June 22-17.

Syer, Capt. Hubert Lionel, London Regt., M.C., Rev. Barrington Blomfield Syer, Rector of Kedington, St. Thomas' Hospital, Nov. 18-16.

Symons, Rev. Charles Fleming Jelinger, R. Welsh Fusiliers, Rev. Jelinger Edward Symons, of Dulwich, Loos, Sept. 25-15.

Symons, 2d. Lt. Charles Handley Lanphier, Royal Fusiliers, Archdeacon Symons, of Shanghai, Nov. 20-17.

Symons, 2d. Lt. Eric Clarence, M.G.C., Archdeacon Symons, of Shanghai, Sept. 1-16.

Talbot, 2d. Lt. Claude Eustace Chetwynd, Somerset L.I., Rev. Percival Burney Talbot, Vicar of Gt. Abington, Sept. 25-15.

Talbot, Lt. Gilbert Walter Lyttelton, Rifle Brigade, Bishop of Winchester, Hooge, July 30-15.

Tanner, Capt. John Champain, R.A.F., Rev. Maurice Tanner, Rector of Eversley, Cranwell, Aug. 1-18.

Tavener, 2d. Lt. Arthur Frederick, K.O.L.I., Rev. Frederick John Winder Tavener, Rector of Wing, Meoutte, Oct. 11-16.

Taylor Charles, Gerald, Engineer Capt., R.N., M.V.O., Rev. Alfred Lee Taylor, Vicar of Ruabon, H.M.S. Tiger, Jan. 24-15.

Taylor, Capt. Ernest Albert Isaac, R.F.A., Rev. Isaac John Taylor, Vicar of Linstead, Janes, July 23-18.

Taylor, 2d. Lt. Maurice Llewelyn, Rifle Brigade, Rev. J. Taylor, Albert, Aug. 26-16.

Taylor, Rev. George Robert Taylor, Vicar of St. Michael's, Byker.

Teape, 2d. Lt. Charles Lewarne, Devonshire Regt., Rev. Charles Richard Teape, Vicar of St. Michael's, Devonport, Guichy, Sept. 4-16.

Temple, Capt. Arthur Hilliard Williams, Suffolk Regt., Mentioned in Despatches, Rev. Robert Charles Temple, Rector of Thorpe Morieux, Kemmel, Dec. 14-14.

Tennant, 2d. Lt. Oswald Moncrieff, West Yorks, Rev. Robert Percy Trevor Tennant, Vicar of Acomb, Ypres, June 16-15.

Theobald, Capt. Frederick George, Royal Lancaster Regt., Rev. Frederick Theobald, Rector of Gt. Wigborough, Le Cateau, Aug. 26-14.

Thicknesse, Lt.-Col. John Audley, Somerset L.I., Bishop Thicknesse, Somme, July 2-16.

Thicknesse, Major Francis William, R.A., D.S.O., Prebendary Thicknesse, Rector of St. George's, Hanover Square, Passchendale, Oct. 19-17.

Thomas, Capt. Greville Wynn, Gurkha Rifles, Rev. Llewellyn Wyn Thomas, Vicar of Newland, El Kefr, Palestine, Apr. 10-18.

Thomas, 2d. Lt. Eric Hand, Duke of Wellington's Regt., Rev. Llewellyn Wyn Thomas, Vicar of Newland, Monchy, Dec. 8-17.

Thomas, 2d. Lt. Thomas Oliver, R. Welsh Fusiliers, Rev. David Pritchard Thomas, Recctor of Llanberis, Mametz Wood, July 11-16.

Thompson, Lt. Charles John McKinnon, Northumberland Fusiliers, Rev. Samuel McKinnon Thompson, Vicar of Northallerton, St. Eloi, March 27-16

Thompson, Lt. Francis Clement, R.F.A., Rev. George Thompson, of Brighton, Ypres, Oct. 3-17.

Thompson, Lt. Horace Brockbank, M.C., Berkshire Regt., Rev. Jacob Thompson, of St. John's College, Colombo, Lake Doiran, Apr. 24-17.

Thompson, Lt. Morice Bell, Machine Gun Corps, Rev. William Francis Thompson, Vicar of Fyfield, Monchy, May 3-17.

Thorburn, Charles Edward Angus, R.E., Rev. Thomas James Thorburn, of Hastings, Chatham, Oct. 22-18.

Thorburn, Capt. John Morgan, Royal Fusiliers, Rev. William John Thornburn, of Hornsey, N, Messines, Aug. 8-17.

Thorndike, Lt. Francis Herbert, Lincoln Yeomanry, R.F.C., Canon Thorndike, of Rochester, August 17-17.

Thorne, 2d. Lt. Charles Everard, M.C., R.E., Rev. Charles William Thorne, Sec. C.M.S., Bombay, Messines, Aug. 16-17.

Thornton, Archibald Clement, Canadian E.F., Canon Thornton, Rector of Downham, Armentieres.

Thornton, Major Frederick Edward, 105th Mahrattas, Canon Thornton, Rector of Downham

Thornycroft, Capt. Edward Gerald Mylton, Lancaster Regt., Rev. J. Mylton Thornycroft, East Africa, Sept. 12-14.

Tisdall, 2d. Lt. Charles Richard, M.C., Irish Guards, Sept. 15-16.

Tisdall Sub.-Lt. Arthur Waldane St. Clair, R.N.V.R., V.C., Rev. William St. Clair Tisdall, Vicar of St. George's, Deal, Gallipoli, May 6-15,

Tisdall, Lt. John Theodore St. Clair, Liverpool Regt., Rev. William St. Clair Tisdall, Vicar of St. George's, Deal, Guillemont, Aug. 8-16.

Tillard, Capt. Arthur George, Manchester Regt., Rev. James Tillard, of Penshurst, Lcs Trois Maisons, Oct. 20-14.

Tollemache, Capt. Leo Quintus, Mentioned in Despatches, Lincoln Regt., Rev. Ralph William Lyonel Tollemache, Rector of South Witham, Belguim, Nov 1-14,

Tollemache, Capt. Leone Sextus, Mentioned in Despatches, Leicester Regt., Rev. Ralph William Lyonel Tollemache, Rector of South Witham Albert, Feb. 20-17.

Tomlinson, Lt. Frederick Roger John, South Staffordshire Regt., Rev. Arthur Roger Tomlinson, Vicar of Bolton le Sands, Ypres, Oct. 26-14.

Tompkins, Harold Newham, Australian I.F., Rev. Herbert Chilton Tompkins, Rector of East Woodhay, Polygon Wood, Sept. 26-17.

Tompkins, J, Australian I.F., Oct. -17.

Toms, Rev. Alfred Augustus Toms, Vicar of Flixton.

Totty, Alfred Clinton, Canadian E.F., Rev. Benjamin Totty, Moosehide Mission, Dawson, Yukon, Mont Dury, Sept. 2-18.

Towend, Capt. Francis Whitchurch, R.E., Rev. Alfred John Townend, C.M.F., Bethune, March 29-15.

Treasure, Midshipman Ivor Neil, R.N.V.R., Rev. James Percy Treasure, Vicar of Condover, H.M.S. Tancred, North Sea, Nov. 11-18.

Trefusis, Capt. Arthur Owen, North Lancashire Regt., Bishop of Crediton, La Boiselles, July 7-16.

Trefusis, Capt. Haworth Walter, Northants Regt., Bishop of Crediton, Le Transloy, Nov. 7-16.

Trelawney, Lt. Henry Walter, Duke of Cornwall's L.I., Rev. Francis Edward Trelawney, of Coldrenick, Contour, Oct. 23-15.

Trench, Major Charles Reginald Chenevix, Sherwood Foresters, Rev. Herbert Francis Chenevix Trench, Vicar of St. Peter's, Thanet, Bullecourt March 21-18.

Trevor, Rev. Ernest Wilberforce, C.F., Rev. George Wilberforce Trevor, Rector of Beeford, Nov. 14-16.

Triphook, Major Owen Leech, R.F.A., Rev. John Crampton Triphook, Rector of Little Tey, Baghdad, Apr. 6-19.

Trotter, Claud Handley, R.A.F., Canon Trotter, of Ardrahan, Co. Galway, Hainault Farm, Oct. 13-18.

Tryon, Major George Arthur, M.C., K.R.R.C., Rev. Arthur William Tryon, Vicar of Middle Rasen, Nov. 7-18.

Tucker, Capt. Virgil, Australian I.F., Dean of Ballarat, Bullecourt, Apr. 11-17.

Tuckey, 2nd Lt. James Caulfield, Middlesex Regt., Rev. James Grove White Tuckey, C.F., Aug. 31-16, Bagdad, Mar. 25-17.

Tuke, Hugh Latimer, New Zealand E.F., Archdeacon of Tauranga, N.Z., Gallipoli, June 7-15.

Tunbridge, Lt. Gerald Charles, York & Lancaster Regt., Rev. James Tunbridge, Vicar of Bisbrooke, Bulgaria, Apr. 27-18.

Turner, Arthur, Gloucester Regt., Rev. Thomas Henley Turner, Rector of Chelwood, Darlington, Sept. 9-15.

Turner, 2d. Lt. Eric Walter Carpenter, Hampshire Regt., Canon Turner, Rector of Overton, Ypres, Aug. 9-16.

Turner, 2d. Lt. Edmund Sanctuary, R.G.A., Rev. William Turner, Vicar of Blacktoft, Ypres, Aug. 21-16.

Turner, 2d. Lt. Arthur Charlewood, Rifle Brigade, Fellow of Trinity Coll., Cambridge, Bishop of Islington, Jan. 16-18.

Turner, Lt. Noel Price James, South Wales Borderers, Rev. John James Turner, Vicar of Pentreheglin, Bethune, May 9-15.

Turner, 2d. Lt. Ronald, Artists Rifles, Rev. Robert Stubbs Turner, Vicar of Tirley, Gallipoli, Aug. 15-16.

Turner, 2d. Lt. Richard Radford, Sussex Regt., Rev. Richard Turner, Vicar of Barnstaple, Ypres, Feb. 3-17.

Tumour, Lt. Arthur William Winterton, Rifle Brigade, Rev. Arthur Henry Tournour, Vicar of St. Augustine's, Stockport, Loos, Sept. 25-15.

Turton, Lt. Richard Dacre, York & Lancaster Regt., Rev. Zouch Horace Turton, Vicar of St. Mary's, Southtown, Ypres, Sept. 24-17.

Turton, Lt. Zouch Austin, Norfolk Regt., Rev. Zouch Horace Turton, Vicar of St. Mary's, Southtown, Ypres, Apr. 23-15.

Tuttiett, Capt. Laurence William, R. Sussex Regt., Rev. Laurence Rayner Tuttiett, Rector of Kelvedon Hatch, Beaumont Hamel, Sept. 3-16.

Tyndale, William Dallas Annesley, Dublin Fusiliers, Rev. William Earle Tyndale, of Horfield, Salonika, March 1-17.

Tyrer, 2d. Lt. Christopher St. John, Royal Warwickshire Regt., Rev. Frank Tyrer, Vicar of Moxley, July 22-16.

Tyson, Capt. Alexander Baird, Argyll & Sutherland Highlanders, Rev. Henry Tyson, Vicar of Cheadle Hulme, Henin, Apr. 23-17.

Uniacke, Col. Robie Fitzgerald, Mentioned in Despatches, Royal Inniskilling Fusiliers, Rev. Robert Fitzgerald Uniacke, Vicar of Tandridge, France, May 17-15.

Upcher, Lt. Sydney, R.N., Canon Upcher, Vicar of Hingham, H.M.S. Vanguard, July 9-17.

Upstone, 2d. Lt. Cedric Donovan, Devonshire Regt., Rev. Philip Upstone, Vicar of Coaley, Bombay, July 11-16.

Urquhart, Capt. Edward Frederick Maltby, Black Watch, Rev. Edward William Urquhart, Vicar of King's Sutton, Pittern, Oct. 23-14.

Usher, Lt. Christopher Lancelot, Wilts Regt., Rev. Robert Usher, Rector of Fovant, Damery, April 23-18.

Ussher, Major, Beverly, Leinster Regt., Rev. Richard Ussher, Vicar of Westbury, Gallipoli, June 22-15.

Ussher, Capt. Stephen, 129th D.C.O. Baluchis, Rev. Richard Ussher, Vicar of Westbury, Givenchy, Dec. 16-14.

Ussher, Lt.-Com. Richard, R.N., D.S.O., Mentioned in Despatches, Rev. Richard Ussher, Vicar of Westbury, Ventnor, Sept. 10-22.

Vallancey, Capt. William Bertram, South African Infantry, Rev. John Vallancey, Vicar of Rosliston, Wynberg, May 17-17.

Vallings, Sub. Lt. Ranulph Kingsley Joyce, R.N.A.S., Rev. James Frederick Vallings, Vicar of Sopley, Struma Front, Jan. 13-17.

Vance, 2d. Lt. Charles Richard Griffin, Cheshire Regt., Chancellor Vance, of Newcastle, Co. Limerick, Ypres, March 9-15.

Vardy, 2d. Lt. Albert Theodore, Warwickshire Regt., Rev. Albert Richard Vardy, Headmaster of King Edward's School, Birmingham, Mametz Wood, July 4-16.

Vaughan, Capt. Robert Wiliam Walter, R.A.M.C., Rev. Thomas Walter Vaughan, Vicar of Rhuddlan, Arras, May 23-17.

Vawdrey, 2d. Lt. Gilbert Lloyd, Welsh Regt., Rev. Llewelyn Brookes Vawdrey, Vicar of Tushingham, Ypres, Nov. 10-17.

Venning, Capt. Edwin Gerald, Suffolk Regt., Rev. Edwin James Venning, Chaplain at Cassel, Ypres, Aug. 6-15.

Vernon, 2d. Lt. Roger, Somerset L.I., Rev. Frederick Wentworth Vernon, of Rangeworthy, Fricourt, May 14-16.

Verso, Capt. Cyril Linton, A.I.F., Canon Verso, Vicar of Berrigan, New South Wales, Zillebehe, Sept. 19-17.

Vivian, Charles Broderick Hugh, Canadian E.F., Rev. Charles Henry Gerald Vivian, Rector of Grade, Amiens, Apr. 3-18.

Vyvyan, Capt. William Geoffrey, Royal Welsh Fusiliers, Rev. Herbert Francis Vyvyan, Rector of Withiel, Zonnebeke, Oct. 24-14.

Wade, Capt. Graham Hardy, Argyll & Sutherland Highlanders, Rev. George Wade, St. Julien, Apr. 25-15.

Waldegrave, 2d. Lt. Edmund John, R.F.A., Rev. Samuel Edmund Waldegrave, Rector of Osborne, Arras, May 10-18.

Waldy, 2d. Lt. Cuthbert Temple, South Lancashire Regt., Rev. Arthur Garmondsway, Waldy, Rector of Yarm, Lorgies, Oct. 20-14.

Wait, Lt. Charles Frederick Wells, King's Own Yorkshire L.I., Rev. Frederick William Wait, Rector of Hasketon, Somme, July 15-16.

Wait, Midshipman Percy Arthur Wells, R.N., Rev. Frederick William Wait, Rector of Hasketon, H.M.S. Queen Mary, Jutland, May 31-16.

Walford, Capt. Hamilton Stewart, Worcestershire Regt., Rev. Walter Shirley Walford, Rector of Sproatley, France, May 27-18.

Walker, 2d. Lt. Claud Arthur Leonard, Inniskilling Fusiliers, Rev. Dr. Walker, Rector of St. Matthew's, Belfast, France, July 11-16.

Walker, 2d. Lt. Edmund Basil, West Kent Regt., Rev. George Sherbrooke Walker, Rector of March, Hill 60., Apr. 18-15.

Walker, Capt. Edward William, D.S.O., Royal Welsh Fusiliers, Rev. William Greaves Walker, Rector of Knockin, Gaza, Nov. 6-17.

Walker, Lt. John West, West Lincolns, Canon Walker, Rector of Barkston, Hargicourt, Apr. 11-17.

Walker, 2d. Lt. Maurice John Lea, R. West Kent, Rev. John William Walker, Vicar of Saxthorpe, May 3-17.

Walker, 2d. Lt, Reginald Fydell, Manchester Regt., Rev. David Walker, Vicar of Darlington, Les Trois Maisons, Oct. 21-14.

Wallace, Capt. Alexander Moultrie, Northants Regt., Rev. Walter Edward Wallace, of Southleigh, Neuve Chapelle, March 12-15.

Wallace, Lt. Cyril Walter, 47th Sikhs, Rev. Walter Edward Wallace, of Southleigh, Kut, March 8-16.

Walley, Lt. Geoffrey Stephen, K.R.R.C., Rev. Stephen Cawley Walley, Rector of Hardingham, Somme, Aug. 20-16.

Walters, 2d. Lt. Edward Charles, Gloucester Regt., Rev. Frank Bridgman Walters, Fellow of Queen's College, Cambridge, France, Dec 22-14.

Walters, Lt. Ernest Beauchamp, Gloucester Regt., Rev. George Ernest Walters, Vicar of Keynsham, Somme, July 30-16.

Walters, Lt. Lancelot John Barrington, R.N., Rev. Charles Barrington Walters, Rector of Sywell, H.M.S. Partridge, Dec. 12-17.

Walton, Lt. Joseph Cyril, West Riding Regt., Rev. John Maxon Walton, Vicar of Southowram, Kemmel, Hill, Apr. 29-18.

Ward, Capt. Arthur Edward Martyr, Norfolk Regt., Rev. J. Martyr Ward, Rector of Gressenhall, Gallipoli, Aug, 12-15.

Ward, Lt. Aubrey Parker Orde, Lincolnshire Regt., Rev. Frederick William Orde Ward, of Eastbourne, Grantham, Nov. 11-18.

Ward, 2d. Lt. Noel Loftus Moore, Essex Regt., Rev, Charles James Ward, Rector of Barnston, Gudecourt, Oct. 15-16.

Ward, 2d. Lt. William Arthur Bayford Kirwan, R.E., Mentioned in Despatches, Rev. William Hallowes Kirwan Ward, Vicar of Asthall, Poperinghe, Aug. 2-15.

Warded, Major Warren Henry, Garkwell Rifles, Rev. Arthur Francis Gregson Warded, of Jubbulpore, Steenwerck, -15.

Warlow, Lt. Edmund Jarvis Leith, Worcester Regt., Archdeacon of Lahore, Somme, Nov. 5-16.

Warlow, Lt. Theodore William, Yorkshire Regt., Rev. George Edmund Warlow, Vicar of Ledsham, Boulogne, July 28-15.

Warren, Major Richard Dunn, Leicester Regt., Rev. Charles Warren, Vicar of St. Michael's, Lincoln, Ypres, Apr. 7-18.

Warren, Capt. James Lionel East, R. Welsh Fusiliers, Rev. John Alexander Faris Warren, C.M.S., Allahabad, Loos, Oct. 2-15.

Warren, 2d. Lt. Theodore Stewart Wolton, Durham L.I., Rev. Charles Theodore Warren, Rector of Chilthorne Domer, Pozieres, July 17-16.

Waters, Capt. George Thorold, Suffolk Regt., Rev. Thomas Waters, Rector of Staverton, Albert, March 29-18.

Waters, 2d. Lt. Kenneth Selby, Indian Army Reserve, Rev. Samuel George Waters, Vicar of Merriden, Murree, May 30-17.

Wayet, Lt. Frank Merewettor, Cameronians, Rev. Frank Field Wayet, Vicar of Pinchbeck, Loos, Sept, 27-15.

Weatherhead, Capt. George Ernest, Lancaster Regt., Canon Weatherhead, Vicar of Seacombe, Ypres, May 8-15.

Weatherhead, Capt. Andrew, Lancaster Regt., Canon Weatherhead, Vicar of Seacombe, Beaumont Hamel, July 1-16.

Webb, Lt.-Com. Arthur Cyril Brooke, R.N.R., Rev. A. Brooke Webb, Jan. 13-18.

Webber, Frederick William, Canadian E.F., Rev. George Henry Webber, Rector of St. Mary's, Port Glasgow, St. Eloi, Apr. 16-15.

Webster, 2d. Lt. Aubrey Herbert Bowen, Northants Regt., Rev. John Webster, Vicar of Ombersley, Albert, Apr. 25-18.

Weekes, 2d. Lt. Walter, Lincoln Regt., Rev. William Harvie Weekes, of Devizes, Scarpe, Apr. 23-17.

Weekes, Harold, Somerset L.I., Rev. William Harvie Weekes, of Devizes, France, March 23-18.

Welchman, Lt. Eric Llewellyn, Lincolnshire Regt., Canon Welchman, of Clifton, Frameries, Aug. 24-14.

Were, Rev. Cyril Narramore, C.F., Bishop of Derby. Jan. 9-18.

Westmacott, 2d. Lt. Frederick Charles, R. West Kent, Canon Westmacott, of Truro, Ypres, July 31-17.

Westmacott, Lt. Spencer Ruscombe, Leinster Regt., Canon Westmacott, of Truro, Ypres, May 8-15.

Whaley, 2d. Lt. Oswald Stanley, Hampshire Regt., Rev. Oswald Whaley, of Bexhill, Gallipoli, Aug. 10-15.

Whall, 2d. Lt. Edward Lionel Haversham, K.R.R.C., Rev. Edward Haversham Whall, Rector of North Barsham, Menin, Sept. 20-17.

Wharton, Herbert, Royal Fusiliers, M.M., Rev. Arthur Patteson Wharton, of Brighton, Delville Wood, July 27-16.

Wheelhouse, 2d. Lt. George William, A.S.C., Rev. George Wheelhouse, Vicar of St. Michael's, Appleby, Mesopotamia, July 6-17.

Widborne, Lt. George Ferris, M.C., Coldstream Guards, Rev. George Ferris Whidborne, Vicar of St. George's, Battersea, Bethune, Oct. 24-15.

Whitaker, Capt. Arthur Cecil, West Yorkshire Regt., Rev. Charles Probart Whitaker, Vicar of Broadclyst, Armentieres, Jan. 1-16.

Whitchurch, Capt. Leslie Sedgwick, 21st I. Cavalry, Rev. Walter Beaumont Gurney Whitchurch, Rector of Spixworth, Messines, Oct. 31-14.

White, 2d. Lt. Gerald John Davis, R. Irish Regt., Bishop of Limerick, Mametz, July 5-16.

White, Capt. Hill Wilson, R.A.M.C., Bishop of Limerick, Vieux Berquin, Apr. 12-18.

White, Reginald Bayley, Bishop of Newfoundland, Etaples, Jan. 9-18.

White, 2d. Lt. Cecil Wilson Morton, Norfolk Regt., Rev. Wilson Woodhouse White, Rector of Brockdish, Loos, Sept. 26-15.

White, 2d. Lt. Robert Stewart, R.F.A., Bishop of Honan, China, Chelsea Hospital, Nov. 4-18.

White, Major William Hawtrey, Royal Irish Regt., Rev. James White, Vicar of St. Peter's, Paddington, St. Eloi, Feb. 14-15.

White, Lt. Hugh Reginald, Middlesex Regt., Rev. Cecil Edward White, Vicar of Holy Trinity, Sloane St., Berry au Bac, May 27-18.

Whitehouse, Major Augustine George Richard, M.C., Herefordshire Regt., Rev. George Whitehouse, Vicar of Sellack, Oulchy, Aug. 1-18.

Whiteside, Capt. Carrol Herbert Marston, Border Regt., Rev. Joseph Whiteside, Rector of Plumstead, Somme, Nov. 1-16.

Whiteside, Capt. Miles Bruce Dalzell, M.C., A.D.C. to Governor of Burmah, Rev. Miles Whiteside, of Hereford, Napsbury, June 13-18.

Whitfeld, Lt. Arthur Noel, Royal Irish Rifles, Rev, Arthur Lewis Whitfeld, Vicar of Hughenden, Bethune, Oct. 14-14.

Whittingham, Lt. Thomas, Leicestershire Regt., Archdeacon of Oakham, Hohenzollern Redoubt, Oct. 13-15.

Whittingstall, Lt. George Herbert Fearnley, Northumberland Fusiliers, Rev. Herbert Oakes Fearnley Whittingstall, Rector of Chalfont St. Giles, Albert, Aug. 3-16.

Wickham, Lt. Bernard William Theodore, M.C., South Staffordshire Regt., Rev. William Arthur Wickham, Rector of Ampton, Ypres, Apr. 13-17.

Wickham, Lt. Anthony Theodore Clephane, Connaught Rangers, Rev. James Douglas Clephane Wickham, of Holcombe Manor, Bath, Ypres, Nov. 2-14.

Wilberforce, Capt. William Robert Sargent, K.R.R.C., Bishop of Chichester, Uphavon, June 2-18.

Wilcock, Lt. Henry Blamires, Essex Regt., Rev. William Henry Wilcock, Rector of Tolleshunt Knights, Beaumont Hamel, Nov. 13-16.

Wilcox, 2d, Lt. Kenneth Theodore Dunbar, R. West Surreys, Rev. Alfred George Wilcox, Vicar of St. George, Battersea, Ypres, Nov. 8-15.

Wilder, 2d. Lt. Reginald Phillips Connor, Suffolk Regt., Rev. William Burnard Chichester Wilder, Rector of Great Bradley, Wulvergham, Nov. 18-14.

Wilford, 2d. Lt. Lionel Russell, Royal Fusiliers, Rev. Herbert Hignett Wilford, Rector of Welney, Marseilles, Nov. 8-18.

Wilkinson, Edward Parker, R.A.M.C., Rev. Robert Parker Wilkinson, Rector of Longparish, Mesopotamia, Oct. 13-18.

Wilkinson, Lt. Francis Dudley, M.C., The Buffs, Mentioned in Despatches, Rev. Dudley Wilkinson, Vicar of Cumnor, Aden, Apr. 19-20.

Wilkinson, George Jerrard, Middlesex Regt., Rev. Willoughby Balfour Wilkinson, Vicar of St. Luke's, Birmingham, Somme, July 1-16.

Wilkinson, Lt. John Rothes Marlow, Middlesex Regt., Rev. Henry Marlow Wilkinson, Vicar of Milford on Sea, Mons, Aug. 23-14.

Willan, Capt. Stanhope Douglas, South Staffordshire Regt., Rev. John Alfred Percy Douglas Willan, Rector of Morley, Miraumont, Feb. 17-17.

Willett, 2d. Lt. Richard, Lancashire Fusiliers, Rev. Richard Knight Willett, Vicar of Norden, Messines, July 31-17.

Williams, 2d. Lt. Arthur Llewelyn, Royal Welsh Fusiliers, Rev. John Williams, of Holyhead, Gaza, March 26-17.

Williams, Capt. Cecil, M.C., Sherwood Foresters, Rev. Hugh Robert Williams, of Ripon, France, March 24-18.

Williams, Lt. Donald Arthur Addams, South Wales Borderers, Rev. Herbert Addams Williams, Rector of Llangibby, Gallipoli, Aug. 11-15.

Williams, Lt. Edmund Oswald Griffith, R. Welsh Fusiliers, Rev. John Meyrick Williams, Rector of Beaumaris, Gibraltar, May 7-16.

Williams, Francis Vivian, S. African F., Mentioned in Despatches, Rev. Benjamin Williams, Rector of Bilborough, Filibusi, Nov. 6-18.

Williams, 2d. Lt. Howard Glynne, K.R.R.C., Rev. Griffith Williams, Rector of Llanrwst, Corwen, Jan. 5-17.

Williams, Noel Griffith, Liverpool Scottish, Rev. Griffith Williams, Rector of Llanrwst, Festubert, Apr. 9-18.

Williams, Harold Penny Garnons, London Regt., Rev. Arthur Garnons Williams, of Abercamlais, Passchendale, Oct. 30-17.

Williams, Surgeon Percy, R.N., Rev. Arthur Garnons Williams, of Abercamlais, H.M.S. Hampshire, June 5-16.

Williams, John Basil Percy, R.E., Rev. William Rhys Williams, Vicar of Param, Antigua W.I., France, June 3-17.

Williams, John Rayner, Shropshire Yeomanry, Rev. John Williams, Rector of St. Margaret's, Port of Spain, West Indies, Trinidad, Sept. 19-18.

Williams, 2d. Lt. Keith, N.Z.E.F., Rev. Alfred Owen Williams of Wanganui, N.Z., Messines, June 8-17.

Williams, 2d. Lt, Timothy Davies, R.G.A., Rev. Charles David Williams, Varennes, March 21-18.

Williams, Capt. Wynne Austin Guest, R. Berkshire Regt., Rev. Samuel Blackwell Guest Williams, Vicar of Pittingham, Sept. 25-15.

Williams, Lt. James William, Canadian E.F., Bishop of Quebec, France, Nov. 18-16.

Williamson, 2d. Lt. Alan Kennedy, Argyll & Sutherland Highlanders, Rev. Henry Lawrence Williamson, April 20-17.

Willink, Capt. Harman James Lindanale, W. Riding Regt., Rev. Arthur Willink, Vicar of Nackington, Vallenciennes, Nov. 5-18.

Willis, William Bryan de Laval, New Zealand E.F., Archdeacon of Waikato, N.Z., Alexandria, May 12-15.

Wilmot, Henry Cecil, Worcester Regt., Rev. Francis Edmund William Wilmot, Rector of Monnington, Lewisham, July -17.

Wilmot, Capt. Robert Conishy, Sherwood Foresters, Rev. Francis Edmund William Wilmot, Rector of Monnington, Poelcappelle, Oct. 29-17.

Wilmot, 2d. Lt. Thomas Norbury M.C., Worcester Regt., Rev. Francis Edmund William Wilmot, Rector of Monnington, Thiepval, Aug. 25-16.

Willmott, Capt. John Herbert Victor, M.C., Essex Regt., Rev. Henry Herbert Willmott, Rector of Rivenhall, Arras, March 28-18.

Wilson, Arthur Shannon, West Yorkshire Regt., Rev. Charles Usher Wilson, Vicar of Sutterton, Achieux, June 11-18.

Wilson, Capt. Charles Edgar Andrew, R.A.M.C., Rev. Alfred Wilson, Vicar of St. Michael's, Chiswick, Etretat, Apr. 8-18.

Wilson, 2d. Lt. Edward, S. African E.F., Canon Wilson, of Worcester, Steenwerck, May 25-16.

Wilson, 2d. Lt. Hugh Stanley, Worcestershire Regt., Canon Wilson, of Worcester, Hebuterne, Sept. 15-15.

Wilson, 2d. Lt. Henry Foss, M.G.C., Rev. William Henry Thomas Wilson, of Clifton, March 21-18.

Wilson, Capt. James Ernest Studholme, M.C., R.A.M.C., Rev. Studholme Wilson, Rector of Millbrook, Poperinghe, Aug. 23-17.

Wilson, Lt. Thomas Percival Cameron, Sherwood Foresters, Rev. Theodore Cameron Wilson, Vicar of Little Eaton, Hermies, March 23-18.

Winch, Harold, Forbes Clarke, Australian I.F., Rev. George Thomas Winch, Vicar of Brompton, Gallipoli, Aug. 6-15.

Winckley, 2d. Lt. Charles Reginald, Sherwood Foresters, Rev. Charles Richard Thorold Winckley, Vicar of Billingborough, Trones Wood, July 20-16.

Windle, Lt. Michael William Maxwell, Devonshire Regt., Rev. William Henry Windle, Rector of Welton, Loos, Sept. 26-15.

Wiseman, Lt. Philip Henry Franklin, North Lancashires, Rev, Henry John Wiseman, of Clifton College, Ypres, Oct. 27-17.

Wiseman, Capt. Willingham Gell Franklin, Lincolnshire Regt., Rev. Henry John Wiseman, of Clifton College, Somme, July 9-16.

Wodehouse, Capt. Arthur Poyys, 123rd Baluchis, Mesopotamia, Nov. 22-15.

Wodeman, Bertram Howard, R.N., Fleet Paymaster, Rev. Henry Wodeman, Vicar of Peckforton, H.M.S. Benbow, Scapa Flow, March 30-18.

Wollocombe, 2d. Lt. Francis, Devonshire Regt., Rev John Henry Bidlake Wollocombe, Rector of Stowford, Corbie, Sept. 10-16.

Wood, Capt. Cecil Strachan, East Yorkshire Regt., Canon Wood, of Rochester, Havre, Dec. 2-14.

Wood, Christopher Eric,

Wood, 2d. Lt. Frank, Sherwood Foresters, Rev. James Hathorn Roworth Wood, Vicar of Cropwell Bishop, St. Omer, Oct. 23-17.

Wood, Rev. Herbert William, C.F., R.G.A., Vicar of Norton, Rev. Thomas Wood, Rector of St. John's, Clerkenwell,

Wood, William Harold, N.Z.E.F., Rev. William Charles Wood, Vicar of Papakura, N.Z., Rouen, Sept. 4-18.

Woodhall, Lt. John F., M.C., M.G.C., Rev. John Duckett Woodhall, Vicar of St. Margaret's, Halliwell, Bolton, Palestine, Nov. 8-17.

Woodhouse, Rev. Disney Charles, Rev. Arthur Chorley Woodhouse, Rector of Winterbourne Monkton, Boulogne, Oct. 6-16.

Woodhouse, Lt. Reginald Courtenay Hulton, 56 Punjabis, Rev. Reginald Illingworth Woodhouse, Rector of Merstham, Mesopotamia, Jan. 14-16.

Woodruff, Lt. Arthur Hamilton Winthrop, Dorset Regt., Rev. Arthur William Woodruff, Rector of North Waltham, Ramadie, Sept. 29-17.

Woods, Lt. Joseph Eric, West Yorkshires, Rev. Francis Henry Woods, Rector of Bainton, Poelcappelle, Oct. 9-17.

Woodward, Lt. Ernest Harold Hamley, West Surrey Regt., Rev. Alfred Ernest Woodward, Vicar of Ugley, Vierstraat, Dec. 24-16.

Woodward, Capt. Edward Seymer, 97th Infantry, Indian Army, Rev. Richard Salisbury Woodward, Vicar of All Saints, Eastbourne, Kut, Jan. 6-16.

Woolley, Alfred Duncan, Essex Regt., Rev. Alfred Duncan Woolley, Rector of Weston Patrick, Midhurst, May 1-18.

Wordsworth, Capt. Alexander Gerald, Middlesex Regt., Rev. John Wordsworth, Vicar of All Hallows, Mealsgate, Laventie, Dec. 6-14.

Wordsworth, Lt. Osmond Bartle, Oxford & Bucks L.I., Rev. Christopher Wordsworth, Sub Dean of Salisbury, Arras, Apr. 2-17.

Worthington, Capt. Tudor Ceitho, South Wales Borderers, Rev. David Worthington, Vicar of Llangeitho, Poix de Nord, Oct. 29-18.

Wray, Capt. Kenneth George Christopher, South Lancashire Regt., Rev. George Daniel Wray, Rector of Easton Grey, Aug. 10-16.

Wrigley, Capt. Willoughby Thornton, M.C., Wilts Regt., Mentioned in Despatches, Rev. Daniel Wrigley, Vicar of Hartburn, Shahraban, Aug. -20.

Wyatt, Col. Arthur Thomas Elford, Lincolnshire Regt., Rev. William Wyatt, Rector of Broughton, London, Feb. 19-17.

Wyatt, Capt. Felix, R.A.F., Rev. James Deen Keriman Mahomed, Rector of Ingham. Changed his name to Wyatt. Gouzeaucourt, July 2-17.

Wyld, Capt., George Richard, Wilts Regt., Canon Wyld, Vicar of Melksham, Givenchy, Dec. 24-14.

Wyllie, Rev. Robert Augustus Platel, Rev. Robert Wyllie, of St. Peter's, Canterbury, Hirano Maru, Nov. 4-18.

Wynne, Capt. Edward Ernest, Leicestershire Regt., Rev. Edward Horace Wynne, Rector of Guestling, Lieven, June 8-17.

Yate, Major Charles Allix Lavington, V.C., Yorkshire L.I., Rev. George Edward Yate, Prebendary of Hereford, Le Cateau, Aug. 26-14.

Young, Major Arthur Hamilton, Winipeg Rifles, Archdeacon Young, of London, Ontario, Arras, Sept. 7-18.

Young, Lt. Robert Percival, M.C., Sussex Regt., Rev. Arthur Frederick Young, Vicar of St. Luke's, Brighton, Jerusalem, Dec. 17-17.

DAUGHTERS

Braithwaite, Margaret Dorothea, Rev, Francis Joseph Braithwaite, Rector of Gt. Waldingfield, Wandsworth Hospital, Mar. 2-19.

Forneri, Agnes Florian, Canon Forneri, of Ontario, Bramshott Hospital, April 21-18.

Phillips, Agnes Clementina, Archdeacon of Furness, St. Thomas' Hospital, S.W., Dec. 24-18.

Shaw, Ellen Miriam Havergal, Rev. William Henry Shaw, Rector of Stapleton, Bedford Hospital, Jan. 15.

Smyth, Mary Grace, Rev. Arthur Worsley Smyth, Vicar of Wymynswold, Isleworth Hospital, Feb. 22-19.

NAVAL CHAPLAINS

Surname.   Christian Name.

Alexander, Philip George. Hampshire. June 5-16.
Back, Hatfield Arthur William. Vanguard. July 9-17.
Browning, Guy Arrott. Indefatigable. May 31-16.
Creed, Algernon Henry George. Orvieto. May 21-17.
Dathan, Joseph Duncan. Pembroke. January 7-18.
Ford, William Lewis. Suffolk. May 9-18.
Greig, George Anthony. Russell, Malta. April 28-16.
Hall, William. Agamemnon. November 4-16.
Hewetson, George Hayton. Bulwark. November 24-14.
Kewney, George Stanley. Queen Mary. May 31-16.
Lewis, Ivor Morgan. Goliath. May 13-15.
Lydall, Cecil Wykeham. Lion. May 31-16.
Milner, Dermond Ross. Garth Castle. September 17-19.
Morgan, George William Faulconer. Invincible. May 31-16.
Patourel, Wallace Mackenzie Le. Defence. May 31-16.
Pitt, Arthur Henry John. Good Hope. November 1-14.
Robinson, George Brooke. Formidable. January 1-15.
Robson, Edward Gleedhall Uphill. Aboukir. September 22-14.
Sweet, Algernon Sidney Osborne. Natal. December 30-15.
Walton, Cyril Ambrose. Chester. May 31-16.
Webber, William Farel. Black Prince. May 31-16.
Wright, Henry Dixon, M.V.O. Barham. May 31-16.

ARMY CHAPLAINS

Surname.   Christian Name.

Abbot, William David, Dieppe, Dec. 3-18.

Acton, Armar Edward, Border Regt., Nov. 4-17.

Ainley, Frederick William, Wimereux, Dec. 5-18.

Ainley, William Preston, Uffington, Oct. 12-15.

Aldridge, Noel, Cleveland, Transvaal, Aug. 16- .

Baile, George William, Etaples, Jan. 27-18.

Baird, James, Canadian Hospital, Feb. 13-19.

Barker, Edward Walter, Buried in B.M.C., Achiet le Grand. March 18-18.

Bell, Charles Henry M. C. R. Buried in B.M.C., Douchy les Ayettes. Berks Regt., Motenville, Aug. 23-18.

Bennett, Arnold John, M.C., El Arish, Jan. 26-18.

Benton, William, Manchester Regt., Aug. 16- .

Bishop, George Bernard Hamilton, Northumberland Fusiliers, May 27-18.

Blakeway, Philip John Thomas, Ismailia, June 10-15.

Boddington, Vincent Coke, Wokingham, March 13-17.

Botwood, Edward Keightley, Sark.

Brown, Guy Spencer Bryan, N.Z.E.F., Ypres, Oct. 4-17.

Brown, W., Pembroke Lodge Hospital.

Buck, Cyril Bernard Wilson, Leicester Regt., Bellenglize, Sept. 29-18.

Cappell, James Leitch, Royal Scots, Jan. 23-18. Buried in St. Maria Cemetery, Ham.

Chadwick, Walter, East African E.F.

Cheese, Walter Gerard, Lincolns, Rouen, Nov. 7-18.

Cleveland, Frederick Walter, M.C.N., Staffords, Rouen, Oct. 11-18.

Cobham, Elijah, King's African Rifles, Sept. 19-17.

Colborne, Richard Arthur Pell, London Regt., Arras. Buried in Dainville M.C. May 28-18.

Craven, George Edward, Rifle Brigade, Salonika, Dec. 7-18.

Creighton, Oswin, R.F.A., Apr. 15-18.

Dallas, William Loraine Seymour, Sept., 20-17.

Deedes, Canon Arthur Gordon, Brixton, Nov. 29-16.

Dickinson, Harry, London Rifles, Oct. 30-17.

Doudney, Charles Edmund, Oct. 16-15. Buried in Lissenhock B.M.C.

Dugdale, Richard William, M.C., Norfolk Regt., Oct. 24-18.

Duncan, Edward Francis, 103rd Inf. Batt., March 11-17. Faubourg d'Amiens B.M.C.

Dunstan, Sidney, Clipstone, July 16-18.

Duvall, John Richard, Manchester Regt., Salonika, Oct. 6-17. Buried in Raisili B.M.C.

East, Herbert Hinton, Zillebeke, Aug., 5-17.

Edinger, Frank Harrison, At Sea, Glenart Castle, Feb. 26-18.

Edwards, Evan, At Home, Nov. 27-18.

Egan, Pierce John, Alexandria, Apr. 6-16.

Evans, E. W., At Home.

Evans, Geoffrey Maynard, M.C., Aug. 11-17.

Finch, Henry Kingsley, Southbourne, Nov. 11-17.

Fisher, Osmond Phillip, Baghdad.

Freestone, William Herbert, Salonika. Stavra M.C. Dec. 14-16.

Fulford, Reginald Hardwick, Salonika, Dec. 15-16.

Garrett, Charles Harold, Sept. 26-17. Vlamertinghe M.C.

Geare, William Duncan, July 31-17. Vlamertinghe M.C.

Gedge, Basil Johnson, Salonika, Apr. 25-17. Colonial B.M.C., Macedonia.

Gibbs, Edward Reginald, Grenadier Guards, Boisleux au Mont, March 29-18.

Green, Ernest Newham, Salisbury, March, 26-16.

Green, Hugh James Bernard, M.G.C., St. Omer, Dec. 8-18.

Griffith, David Howell, At Home.

Gunson, Henry Edward, Cosham, Aug. 23-18.

Harbord, Frank Robert, Aug. 8-17.

Harding, Wilfred John, M.C., Oct. 31-17.

Hardy, Theodore Bayley, V.C., D.S.O., M.C., Lincoln Regt., Rouen, Oct. 18-18.

Hatfield, Arthur Percival, Armarah, July 9-18.

Hawdon, Noel Eliot, Boulogne, Nov. 16-18.

Heath, Alfred, West Riding Regt., June 30-18. Toulencourt Cemetery.

Henderson, Robert Morley, Feb. 3-19.

Hewitt, Frederick Whitmore, Loos, Sept. 28-15. Vermelles Cemetery.

Hoare, Henry James, Egypt.

Holden, Oswald Addenbrooke, 60th Infantry Brigade, Cambrai, Dec. 1-17.

Hood, Charles Ivo Sinclair, R.G.A., Poperinghe, Apr. 15-18.

Houlston, Edgar Charles, May 4-17. At Sea. Buried at Marseilles.

Howell, Thomas, King's Shropshire L.I., Dec. 1-17.

Hunter, Phillip Needham, Shorncliffe.

Inglis, Rupert Edward, Sept. 18-16. Buried at Gimchy, N.W. of Combles.

Jefferys, Charles Thomas Claude, Chelsea, Nov. 20-18.

Jenkins, D.

Johnson, Ernest Edward, Lancashire Fusiliers, Dec. 1-18.

Jones, Basil, Havre, Oct. 25-18.

Jones, Thomas Glasfryn, S. Wales Borderers, Vincent Square Hos., Apr. 12-17.

Jones, William Edgar, Yorkshire Regt., Oct. 24-18.

Jones, William Evans, R.W. Fusiliers, Oct. 8-18.

Judd, Alan Cecil, M.C., Notts & Derby Regt., March 21-18.

Kay, William Henry, M.C,, Dorset Regt., Apr. 5-18.

Keene, Benjamin Corrie, Sept. 26-17, E. Yorks. Regt.

Langdon, Cecil, Border Regt., Oct. 31-17.

Lawson, Henry Heaton, Northants Regt., March 24-18.

Leakey, Herbert Nettleton, July 24-17

Ledbitter, Herbert Peter, Le Treport, Feb. 28-17.

Lendrum, James Herbert Reginald, Aug. 22-18. Blenvillers M.C.

Lester, Gerald James, Dec 16-18.

Longridge, Archibald Owen Carwithen, Gen. Hos., Boulogne, Oct. 10-18.

Lycett, Bertie, Vicar of Orchards, Johannesburg, March 6-19.

Mace, Alban Bodley, Salonika, Oct. 3-16.

Major, Charles William Wykeham, Euskirchen, March 19-19.

Martyn, Cecil Radcliffe, Rouen, March 3-19.

Meister, Charles Gustave Clark, M.C., Apr. 18-18.

Mitchell, Charles Wand, East Yorkshire Regt., May 3-17. Faubourg d'Amiens Cemetery.

Moore, Edgar Noel, M.C., Liverpool Regt., Ypres, January, 5-18.

O'Connor, W., Hamadan.

O'Rorke, Benjamin Garniss, D.S.O., Falmouth, Dec. 25-18.

Pardoe, George Southey, Jerusalem, Oct. 15-18.

Peel, Hon. Maurice Berkeley, M.C., May 14-17.

Plummer, Charles Benjamin, March 12-17. Garnoy M.C.

Plumptre, Basil Pemberton, M.C., London Regt., March 12-17.

Powell, John William Alcock Eyre, labour Corps, Apr. 16-18.

Pratt, Arthur Morrel, Rouen.

Ranking, George Harvey, Cambrai, Nov. 20-17.

Read, Eric Oswald, Dorset Regt., Oct. 3-18.

Roche, Francis Cavendish, Alexandria, Nov. 14-15.

Schooling, Cecil Herbert, Belgium. Buried in Lissenthock M.C. Poperinghe, June 21-17.

Smith, Frederick Seaton, York and Lancaster Regt., Boulogne, Nov. 15-18.

Smyth, Edward Johnson, Rouen, Feb. 10-17.

Spence, Alexander, M.C., P.O.W., March 31-18. Buried in Ham Cemetery.

Spink, Hubert Octavius, Aug., 9-16. Buried in Dives Copse C.

Staunton, Harvey, Jan. 14-18, Azizieh, Mesopotamia.

Stewart, James Robert, Worcester Regt., Jan. 2-16, Cambrai.

Streeten, Basil Robert, Lancashire Fusiliers, Nov. 1 18. Don. S.W. Lille

Trevor, Ernest Wilberforce, Rifle Brigade, Nov. 14-16.

Tuke, Francis Henry, July 20-16, Montauban.

Vine, Hatton Bertram St. John de, Apr. 27-16. Buried in Vermelles B.M.C.

Wallace, John James, N. Stafford Regt., Nov. 8-18.

Watson, John Edmund Malone, Middlesex Regt., Apr. 10-18.

Were, Cyril Narramore, Jan. 9-18. Buried in Outersteene C.

Wood, Harold William, R.G.A., Vicar of Norton, Nov. 1-18.

Woodhouse, Disney Charles, R. Sussex Regt., Oct. 6-16, Boulogne.

ADDENDA

GENERAL LIST

Kendall, Lt. Locke Francis William Angerstein, Norfolk Regt., Revd. John Francis Kendall, Vicar of Richmond, Jerusalem, 21st November, 1917.

ARMY CHAPLAIN

James Stanley Bromfield Brough, Mentioned in Despatches, Mildmay Head Quarters, 11th November, 1918.